CW00734989

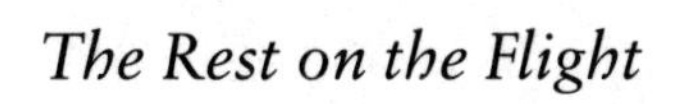

The Rest on the Flight

Also by Peter Porter in Picador

Max is Missing
Afterburner
Better Than God

The Rest on the Flight

Selected Poems

Peter Porter

PICADOR

First published 2010 by Picador
an imprint of Pan Macmillan, a division of Macmillan Publishers Limited
Pan Macmillan, 20 New Wharf Road, London N1 9RR
Basingstoke and Oxford
Associated companies throughout the world
www.panmacmillan.com

ISBN 978-0-330-52218-2

9 8 7 6 5 4 3 2 1

A CIP catalogue record of this book is available from
the British Library.

Typeset by Ellipsis Books Limited, Glasgow
Printed in the UK by CPI Mackays, Chatham ME5 8TD

Contents

Introduction by Sean O'Brien xv

ONCE BITTEN, TWICE BITTEN

Forefathers' View of Failure 5
Mr Roberts 7
All Other Time is Peace 8
Beast and the Beauty 9
John Marston Advises Anger 10
Death in the Pergola Tea-Rooms 12
A Vicious Vignette 14
Annotations of Auschwitz 15
Who Gets the Pope's Nose? 18
Phar Lap in the Melbourne Museum 20
Tobias and the Angel 22

PENGUIN MODERN POETS

Your Attention Please 27
Soliloquy at Potsdam 30
Nine o'Clock Thoughts on the 73 Bus 32
Ghosts 33
Eat Early Earthapples 36
Reading MND in Form 4B 38

POEMS ANCIENT AND MODERN

Vienna 43
Sydney Cove, 1788 45
Madame de Merteuil on 'The Loss of an Eye' 47
The World of Simon Raven 48
Homage to Gaetano Donizetti 49
The Great Poet Comes Here in Winter 50
Encounter in Antioch 52

A PORTER FOLIO

The Last of the Dinosaurs 55
My Late T'ang Phase 57
Fantasia on a Line of Stefan George 58
A Hoplite's Helmet 59
Seahorses 61
Futurity 62
The History of Music from 'Three Poems for Music' 64
Fair Go for Anglo-Saxons 66
The Porter Song Book 71

THE LAST OF ENGLAND

The Last of England 77
A Meredithian Treatment 78
Short Story 79
Diana and Actaeon 81
The Workers 82
A Consumer's Report 84
Stroking the Chin 86

Let Me Bore You with My Slides 89
The Sadness of the Creatures 90
On This Day I Complete My Fortieth Year 93
'The Sanitized Sonnets' 96

PREACHING TO THE CONVERTED

The King of the Cats is Dead 99
Fossil Gathering 101
May, 1945 102
Sex and the Over-Forties 103
Dream Restaurant 104
In the Giving Vein 105
The Dust 107
Mort aux chats 110
Tending towards the Condition 112
Postcard Poems 113
James Joyce Sings 'Il mio tesoro' 116

AFTER MARTIAL

I. xliii 121
II. lii 122
II. lxxxvi 123
III. xii 124
III. xxxv 125
IV. xviii 126
IV. xliv 127
V. lviii 128
VI. xxxix 129

VIII. xxix 131
IX. xxxiii 132
IX. liv 133
XI. xcix 134
XI. civ 135
XII. xviii 138
XII. xxxi 141
XIV. xxxix 142

LIVING IN A CALM COUNTRY

Living in a Calm Country 145
An Australian Garden 146
On First Looking into Chapman's Hesiod 149
Frogs at Lago di Bolsena 152
The Descent into Avernus 153
Dreamtime 155
Cat's Fugue 157
Ode to Afternoon 159
That Depression is an Abstract 162
The Settembrini Waltz 165

THE COST OF SERIOUSNESS

The Picture of Nobody 169
Waiting for Rain in Devon 171
The Easiest Room in Hell 172
An Angel in Blythburgh Church 174
An Exequy 176
The Delegate 180
The Cost of Seriousness 184
Gertrude Stein at Snails Bay 187

The Painters' Banquet 190
Non Piangere, Liù 192
The Lying Art 193
A Lecture by my Books 195
Roman Incident 197

ENGLISH SUBTITLES

My Old Cat Dances 203
Returning 204
Sonata Form: The Australian Magpie 206
What I Have Written I Have Written 208
The Future 210
Alcestis and the Poet 212
Addio Senza Rancor 214
Talking to You Afterwards 216
Pope's Carnations Knew Him 218
Landscape with Orpheus 219

FAST FORWARD

The Flock and the Star 225
Doll's House 226
A Guide to the Gods 228
Dejection: An Ode 229
To Himself 231
Going to Parties 232

THE AUTOMATIC ORACLE

A Sour Decade 237
Throw the Book at Them 238

The Rest on the Flight 240
And No Help Came 242
Pontormo's Sister 243
To Lacedaemon Did My Land Extend 245
Paradis Artificiel 247
Nevertheless 249
The Melbourne General Cemetery 252

POSSIBLE WORLDS

Woop Woop 257
The Ecstasy of Estuaries 259
A Chagall Postcard 261
Civilization and its Disney Contents 262
Little Buddha 264
Frogs Outside Barbischio 266
River Run 267
Serious Drinking 269
An Ingrate's England 270
Copyright Universal Pictures 272
The Orchard in E-Flat 275

THE CHAIR OF BABEL

Bad Dreams in Venice 279
Bad Dreams in Naples 281
Wish We Were There 283
Pigeons, Gulls and Starlings 285
In Rosewell 287
The Chair of Babel 288
Wittgenstein's Dream 291

Listening to Shakespeare 293
A Tour of the City 296
The Cartrac Quatrains 299

MILLENNIAL FABLES

The Approach Road 303
World Poetry Conference Welcome Poem 304
Aesop's Dressing Gown 305
Winckelmann at the Harbourside 307
Berenson Spots a Lotto 308

DRAGONS IN THEIR PLEASANT PALACES

Kings and Messengers 315
Hardy, 1913 316
Old Goldfields, Maryborough 317
The Western Canoe 319
Collateral Damage 321
The Lion of Antonello da Messina 323
The Pines of Rome 324
The Cocks of Campagnatico 326
A Lament 327
Dragons in their Pleasant Palaces 329

BOTH ENDS AGAINST THE MIDDLE

Leaving Mantua 333
Basta Sangue 336
A Honeymoon in 1922 337
Both Ends Against the Middle 339

Jumping Ship 340
To My Granddaughters Sweeping Spelsbury Church 341

MAX IS MISSING

Streetside Poppies 347
Max is Missing 349
A Butterfly Stampede 351
The Last Hours of Cassiodorus 353
So Unimaginably Different and So Long Ago 354
Streamers 355
Tasso's Oak 356
The Philosophers' Garden 358
Magica Sympathia 361
Hermetically Sealed or What the Shutter Saw 363
Deo Gratias Anglia 366
Calumny 367
The Man Who Knew Everybody 369
Ex Libris Senator Pococurante 371

AFTERBURNER

Deuterothanatos 375
The Rider Haggard Window, St Mary's, Ditchingham 376
The Man Who Spoke in Tongues 377
Sex and the Over-Seventies 378
Horace's Odes Translated 379
Rimbaud's Ostrich 381
Afterburner 382
The Last Wave Before the Breakwater 384
In a Time of the Wilting of Poinsettias 385
Stravinsky in Hollywood 387

BETTER THAN GOD

Better Than God 391
The Apprentice's Sorcerer 392
We do Not Write the Way We Are 394
Whereof We Cannot Speak 396
That War is the Destruction of Restaurants 398
A Very Forgiving Medium 399
Leafing Through the Latin Dictionary 401
Voltaire's Allotment 402
In Bed with Oblomov 404
Henry James and Constipation 406
Birds in the Garden of the Cairo Marriott 409
Ranunculus Which My Father Called a Poppy 410
Christmas Day, 1917 411
The Violin's Obstinacy 413
River Quatrains 414
The Downside 416
Opus 77 417

2010

After Schiller 421

Introduction

Much have I travelled in the realms of gold
for which I thank the Paddington and Westminster
Public Libraries: and I have never said sir
to anyone since I was seventeen years old

'THE SANITIZED SONNETS', 4

These, the opening lines of a sonnet from *The Last of England* (1970), the book which confirmed Peter Porter's reputation, condense some significant features of Porter's work and life. Settled in England since 1951, Porter was born in 1929 in Brisbane, Queensland, and shares both the democratic spirit and the cultural hunger which have characterized many Australians. Libraries, the theatre, the concert hall, the opera house and the gallery are often home to Porter's copious imagination. At the same time as he claims this European inheritance, he turns a scorching critical gaze on the apparatus of class and privilege and wealth that can make culture seem like property. Porter's is not a poetry of compartments: sexual resentment and a rapid education in how 'the inheritors are inheriting still' are likely to be found on the same page as meditations and dramatic monologues on art and literature. His satirical impulse is rarely asleep, and he incorporates himself among its objects, for example in his depictions of London as it wakes into the 1960s and an illusory 'democratic sexiness'.

Porter's poetry is urbane, but its assurance is balanced by a powerful anxiety, in which the apprehension of mortality seems fused with a sense of the vulnerability of love. He was nine when his mother died suddenly, and the implacable and peremptory fact of death reaches into all areas of his work. Death, he discovered, 'was a word like "when", / and not a thing like cat.' In *The Cost of Seriousness* (1978) he is the elegist of his first wife, Jannice Henry, in his recasting of Henry King's 'An Exequy' (1657). Elsewhere in the book Jannice herself speaks as a 'delegate' from beyond the grave, explaining that 'What we do . . . is its own parade.'

The consolations of faith are not open to Porter, but throughout his work we find the sense of scale which is the legacy of belief – a sense shared with his two great literary inspirations, Shakes-peare and Browning. It is from them too that he develops his sense of the dramatic and his fondness for monologue and soliloquy begun *in medias res*. Historical and literary figures (Frederick the Great of Prussia, Rilke, Christopher Smart) mingle with characters from fiction and mythology. Having wished for 'fictions to be real in', he also incorporates narrative cross-sections and recastings of other bodies of work (see 'The World of Simon Raven' and 'The Settembrini Waltz'), while his versions of Martial present a metropolitan world of sex and dining and gossip to which the present equivalent bears an ever more marked resemblance.

If for Porter the borders of the real and the imagined are not entirely secure, the traffic between the two has its equivalent in the diversity of his shaping enthusiasms. These encompass the sobriety of middle and later Auden, German Romanticism, Pope but also Rochester, Rilke but on no account Dante. His tastes in art are equally varied (though he comments: 'I'm fond of the overdone') and he favours opera and baroque music. And he writes about all these things, ignoring Kingsley Amis's attempt to prevent poems about other poems and paintings and foreign cities and museums, at the same time annoying those who think poetry should subordinate itself to accessibility. To view Porter as elitist is to miss the point: the constellation of overlapping worlds which his work evokes is open to anyone interested to explore for themselves, and his reflections on art are always connected to its human sources – and to power in various manifestations. In 'Soliloquy at Potsdam' Frederick of Prussia declares:

> I like to think
> That in an afternoon of three sonatas
> A hundred regiments have marched more miles
> Than lie between here and Vienna and not once
> Has a man broken step. Who would be loved
> If he could be feared and hated, yet still
> Enjoy his lust, eat well and play the flute?

Breadth of subject is matched by diversity of form. Porter traverses ode, elegy, satire, lyric, monologue, epistle and numerous stanzas and metres, recalling one of his two great modern masters, Auden (the other is Wallace Stevens). There is a corresponding range of tone and vocabulary – low comedy meets visionary grandeur, elegy is matched by epigram. Poet and poem should, Porter considers, be able to go anywhere, if they keep their wits about them.

Increasingly in his later career Porter has chosen to return to Australia, to consider his own past and the landscapes and history of the 'Boeotian' continent, the New World where 'happiness is enforced'. His long residence in London has led some Australians to consider him disloyal, but Porter is too intelligent to confuse nationalism with love of a homeland, or to simplify that love in order to win approval. The world he depicts is one he finds both familiar and mysterious, summoning a fresh energy into his work in poems such as 'Woop Woop' and 'The Ecstasy of Estuaries'.

The 1989 *Porter Selected* drew on eleven books and some uncollected material and weighed in with ninety-six poems. In 2010 Don Paterson and I have nineteen books, over eight hundred poems, to choose from. The resulting contents would make a substantial *Collected Poems* for many poets. What has struck us is the extraordinary sustained quality of the material: habit has little part in Porter's poetry. And to that should be added that the most recent books have, if anything, shown a gain in intensity. Porter's contemporaries include Ted Hughes and Geoffrey Hill, and the appropriate comparison is with these major poets of the period following 1945. He is as distinctive and memorable as either, and utterly different from both:

> Behind us is the deep note of the universe,
> The E-flat pedal on which time is built,
> Spreading and changing, both a subtle
> Growth of difference and a minimalist
> Phrase, with bridges crossing it and staves
> Of traffic on its tide, a broad bloodstream
> To carry to the delta full mythologies.
>
> 'THE ORCHARD IN E-FLAT'

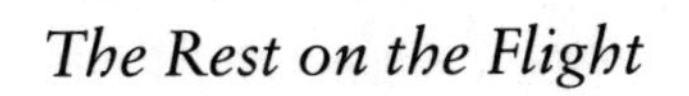

The Rest on the Flight

ONCE BITTEN, TWICE BITTEN

Forefathers' View of Failure

Men with religion as their best technique,
Who built bush churches six days a week,
Stencilled failure's index on their brains.
Whisky laced the mucus of their heads,
Flushed their pores, narrow-bored their veins,
But they were building still on their death-beds
Having no life but the marking-time of work,
Sleeping collapsed outside despair and talk.

These ancestors might pity or despise
Free will, willing despair into lives.
They used sin as a weather-telling limb,
Climbed to bed with a bottle, took
Days on a bender but never had a whim
Like protest or millennium from a book –
These narrow fates had a viciousness
They drank for, but no vicariousness.

It would seem failure to them to have
Knowledge a Scottish textbook never gave
Or to fear regular love on an iron bedstead
With children lying awake a wall away.
Their sophistication was only to be dead
After drinking the sun down into the bay.
Their gulps shake out time, their health
Is in country roses, a hard red wealth.

The weatherboard churches bleached white
As the calcimined crosses round them invite,
Like the War Memorial with ten names,
Eyes up to plain Heaven. It is hard to see
Past good intentions – on any visitor the same
Wind trespasses ashore from a wailing sea.
In this new land the transplanted grasses root,
Waving as sulkily as through old falling soot.

Mr Roberts

He was the great Consul and his teacher's gown
Out-toga'd the forum of his Latin Class.
His eyes translated what they rested on:
Boys of the pudding world, unstoical faces,
Ears beyond the ablative, all thickened glass.
Staring into them he might have drowned
In such transparency – A Roll Call of some spaces –
They wore their fear to match his moral frown.

This pedagogue pushed: he owned them for four years.
A Rugby field was the Republic's mould
Which that soft thing the self so rightly feared.
The gravel rash, the sweaty jersey kept
Faith with the Silver Age, The Men of Old;
Your father stepping from an otiose car,
In the school's shadow as the Speech Day sun crept
Up, felt an ancient fright, a gladiator's jar.

Headmasters dwindle but contrive to last.
Thicker bodies fray than stood the cane.
Later a man shot himself, a man went mad – ask
The secret smoker in the bike shed what
Sour light stood on the school's weather vane,
What Tartarus vented in the boiling Bell Tower
But no revolution came: that comic spot,
The Old School waits and presages each unshining hour.

All Other Time is Peace

What is locked in a book
Of a Civil War, of a king
Watching over the unwalled marshes,
Of disease in the Long Walls awaiting
A hot day, of panic and cold night marches
To cities on heavy plains
Is history which once was done
Congregationally in the sun
For the living who will remain.

While the city burned to the water
And the merchants sailed away,
Murder, the child's friend, wept
The four-sided dead: where are they,
Foul and alone, the well-kept
Of time? Asleep, which is death
And cannot be slept out,
Where they lie mouth to mouth,
Apart, not kept together by breath.

Main peace is worn down
To fear and the glamorous war:
Friend for his friend gives away
That life, his Sanitary Law
He knows he still must obey.
All time is war and all men
Live in the picture of death;
The Heaven and Hell they bequeath
Is old time, old peace again.

Beast and the Beauty

His fear never loud in daylight, risen to a night whisper
Of a dead mother in the weatherboard house,
He had this great piece of luck: a girl
In Paris clothes, ex-school monitor, chose
Him for her lover. Twenty-one and experienced,
She showed his hands the presentiment of clothes
And first at a party kissed him, then took
Him home where they did what he'd always supposed.

Her sophistication was his great delight:
Her mother and father drinking, throwing things,
The unhappy marriage, the tradespeople on Christian
Name terms – all the democratic sexiness – mornings
With the Pick of the Pops and the Daily Express
And yet the sudden itching despair, the wonder in King's
College Chapel, the depth that lived in her soul
Of which this raciness was only the worldly covering.

But the sophistication chose to kill – the itch
Was on the inside of the skin. Her family of drunks
Were shrewd, wine-wise young barristers and gentlemen-
Farmers fought for her hand. In the loft there waited trunks
Of heirlooms to be taken seriously. He found himself
Ditched, his calls unanswered, his world shrunk
To eating in Lyons', waiting outside her house at midnight,
Her serious tears to haunt him, boiling on his bunk.

So he sits alone in Libraries, hideous and hairy of soul,
A beast again, waiting for a lustful kiss to bring
Back his human smell, the taste of woman on his tongue.

John Marston Advises Anger

All the boys are howling to take the girls to bed.
Our betters say it's a seedy world. The critics say
Think of them as an Elizabethan Chelsea set.
Then they've never listened to our lot – no talk
Could be less like – but the bodies are the same:
Those jeans and bums and sweaters of the King's Road
Would fit Marston's stage. What's in a name,
If Cheapside and the Marshalsea mean Eng. Lit.
And the Fantasie, Sa Tortuga, Grisbi, Bongi-Bo
Mean life? A cliché? What hurts dies on paper,
Fades to classic pain. Love goes as the MG goes.
The colonel's daughter in black stockings, hair
Like sash cords, face iced white, studies art,
Goes home once a month. She won't marry the men
She sleeps with, she'll revert to type – it's part
Of the side-show: Mummy and Daddy in the wings,
The bongos fading on the road to Haslemere
Where the inheritors are inheriting still.
Marston's Malheureux found his whore too dear;
Today some Jazz Club girl on the social make
Would put him through his paces, the aphrodisiac cruel.
His friends would be the smoothies of our Elizabethan age –
The Rally Men, Grantchester Breakfast Men, Public School
Personal Assistants and the fragrant PROs,
Cavalry-twilled tame publishers praising Logue,
Classics Honours Men promoting Jazzetry,
Market Researchers married into Vogue.
It's a Condé Nast world and so Marston's was.

His had a real gibbet – our death's out of sight.
The same thin richness of these worlds remains –
The flesh-packed jeans, the car-stung appetite
Volley on his stage, the cage of discontent.

Death in the Pergola Tea-Rooms

Snakes are hissing behind the misted glass.
Inside, there are tea urns of rubicund copper, chromium pipes
Pissing steam, a hot rattle of cups, British
Institutional Thickness. Under a covering of yellowing glass
Or old celluloid, cress-and-tomato, tongue-and-ham
Sandwiches shine complacently, skewered
By 1/6 a round. The wind spitefully lays the door shut
On a slow customer – ten pairs of eyes track
To his fairisle jersey; for a few seconds voices drop
Lower than the skirmishing of steam.
Outside by the river bank, the local doctor
Gets out of his '47 Vauxhall, sucking today's
Twentieth cigarette. He stops and throws it
Down in the mud of the howling orchard.
The orchard's crouching, half-back trees take the wind
On a pass from the poplars of the other bank,
Under the scooping wind, a conveyor-belt of wrinkles,
The buckled river cuts the cramping fields.
Just out of rattle reach and sound of cup clang,
The old rationalist is dying in the Pergola.
Two Labour Party friends and the doctor
Rearrange his woven rugs. The blood is roaring
In his head, the carcinoma commune, the fronde
Of pain rule in his brain – the barricades have broken
In his bowels – it is the rule of spasm, the terror sits.
He knows he is dying, he has a business of wills,
Must make a scaffolding for his wife with words,
Fit the flames in his head into the agenda.
Making up his mind now, he knows it is right

To take the body through committee meetings and
campaign rooms
To wear it and patch it like a good tweed; to come to
The fraying ends of its time, have to get the doctor
To staple up its seams just to keep the fingers
Pulling blankets up, stroking comfort on other fingers,
Patting the warm patch where the cat has been.
There is no God. It is winter, the windows sing
And stealthy sippers linger with their tea.
Now rushing a bare branch, the wind tips up
The baleful embroidery of cold drops
On a spider's web. Inside the old man's body
The draught is from an open furnace door – outside the room,
Ignoring the doctor's mild professional face,
The carnival winter like the careful God
Lays on sap-cold rose trees and sour flower beds
The cruel confusion of its disregard.

A Vicious Vignette

In the trees around the small summerhouse
The birds still raggedly call
In uneven entries, high and shrill and sour.
The custodian in a grey uniform
Shows visitors the room where the great
Symphonies were written; here for hours
While his wife wrote letters and made cakes
The composer put man and nature in a cage
Of furious sound – they raged for him, the powers
Of sickness and life. Critics of our day have shown
His Pantheism in the birdsong in his scores,
More feeling than painting, they say, this
His great mother, Nature, and her song.
The Biographer who came here in winter knows
(Padding about the wind-walled cottage
His grant spent on rococo Austrian treasures and rich food)
That, rising from his desk in the bright house,
The Composer took his gun and broke the Summer,
Shot at the birds calling in the leaves,
Went in then to compose to a silence
Of clangorous birds in his head
Music of his guilty childhood's peace.

Annotations of Auschwitz

1

When the burnt flesh is finally at rest,
The fires in the asylum grates will come up
And wicks turn down to darkness in the madman's eyes.

2

My suit is hairy, my carpet smells of death,
My toothbrush handle grows a cuticle.
I have six million foulnesses of breath.
Am I mad? The doctor holds my testicles
While the room fills with the zyklon B I cough.

3

On Piccadilly underground I fall asleep –
I shuffle with the naked to the steel door,
Now I am only ten from the front – I wake up –
We are past Gloucester Rd, I am not a Jew,
But scratches web the ceiling of the train.

4

Around staring buildings the pale flowers grow;
The frenetic butterfly, the bee made free by work,
Rouse and rape the pollen pads, the nectar stoops.
The rusting railway ends here. The blind end in Europe's gut.
Touch one piece of unstrung barbed wire –
Let it taste blood: let one man scream in pain,
Death's Botanical Gardens can flower again.

5

A man eating his dressing in the hospital
Is lied to by his stomach. It's a final feast to him
Of beef, blood pudding and black bread.
The orderly can't bear to see this mimic face
With its prim accusing picture after death.
On the stiff square a thousand bodies
Dig up useless ground – he hates them all,
These lives ignoble as ungoverned glands.
They fatten in statistics everywhere
And with their sick, unkillable fear of death
They crowd out peace from executioners' sleep.

6

Forty thousand bald men drowning in a stream –
The like of light on all those bobbing skulls
Has never been seen before. Such death, says the painter,
Is worthwhile – it makes a colour never known.
It makes a sight that's unimagined, says the poet.
It's nothing to do with me, says the man who hates
The poet and the painter. Six million deaths can hardly
Occur at once. What do they make? Perhaps
An idiot's normalcy. I need never feel afraid
When I salt the puny snail – cruelty's grown up
And waits for time and men to bring into its hands
The snail's adagio and all the taunting life
Which has not cared about or guessed its tortured scope.

7

London is full of chickens on electric spits,
Cooking in windows where the public pass.
This, say the chickens, is their Auschwitz,
And all poultry eaters are psychopaths.

Who Gets the Pope's Nose?

It is so tiring having to look after the works of God.
The sea will run away
From martyrs' feet, gay
Dissipated Florentines kiss tumours out of a man's head,
Scheduled liquefactions renew saints' blood,

In Andean villages starved Inca girls
Develop the stigmata,
Dying dogs pronounce the Pater
Noster on the vivisection table, the World
Press report trachoma'd eyes that drip wide pearls.

All investigated, all authenticated, all
Miracles beyond doubt.
Yet messengers go in and out,
The Vatican fills up with paper. The faithful
Work for a Merchant God who deals in souls.

Was there ever a man in Nazareth who was King of Kings?
There is a fat man in Rome
To guide his people home.
Bring back the rack and set the bones straining,
For faith needs pain to help with its explaining.

Fill a glass with water and gaze into it.
There is the perfect rule
Which no God can repeal.
Having to cope with death, the extraordinary visit,
Ordinary man swills in a holy sweat.

And high above Rome in a room with wireless
The Pope also waits to die.
God is the heat in July
And the iron band of pus tightening in the chest.
Of all God's miracles, death is the greatest.

Phar Lap in the Melbourne Museum

A masterpiece of the taxidermist's art,
Australia's top patrician stares
Gravely ahead at crowded emptiness.
As if alive, the lustre of dead hairs,
Lozenged liquid eyes, black nostrils
Gently flared, otter-satin coat declares
That death cannot visit in this thin perfection.

The democratic hero full of guile,
Noble, handsome, gentle Houyhnhnm
(In both Paddock and St Leger difference is
Lost in the welter of money) – to see him win
Men sold farms, rode miles in floods,
Stole money, locked up wives, somehow got in:
First away, he led the field and easily won.

It was his simple excellence to be best.
Tough men owned him, their minds beset
By stakes, bookies' doubles, crooked jocks.
He soon became a byword, public asset,
A horse with a nation's soul upon his back –
Australia's Ark of the Covenant, set
Before the people, perfect, loved like God.

And like God to be betrayed by friends.
Sent to America, he died of poisoned food.
In Australia children cried to hear the news
(This Prince of Orange knew no bad or good).
It was, as people knew, a plot of life:
To live in strength, to excel and die too soon,
So they drained his body and they stuffed his skin.

Twenty years later on Sunday afternoons
You still can't see him for the rubbing crowds.
He shares with Bradman and Ned Kelly some
Of the dirty jokes you still don't say out loud.
It is Australian innocence to love
The naturally excessive and be proud
Of a broad-limbed chestnut bay gelding who ran fast.

Tobias and the Angel

When I play the sad music my conscience urges,
I hear through the great summary of our loss
My father praising the long cataract before his eyes
Where on the retina he starves for light.
We are an unlucky family and we have faith
For which we praise our oppressors and our God.

This has been a long journey; my dog is tired,
My companion is a holy dandy, his clothes are praise.
The fish leap from the river, short verbs hold time
For me in a haul – I have an inventory of praise
And do not tire of the simple entering in,
Like my father closing his Day Book on his trade.

There is no justice: love relies on luxury,
Faith on habit, health on chemistry,
But praise sits with persistence. Today
There is a sun pestering the water, tomorrow
A water falling from the sun and always
The pilgrim cursing the falling water and performing sun.

I shall get home one day or if I die instead
An Insurance Angel will tell my waiting wife
His grave is furnished by his good upbringing,
His habits were proper, his doubt all to the good;
From his warm orthodoxy melancholy shrinks,
He did what he was told, obedient and sane.

So when the miracle strikes from the open door,
The scales fall from my father's eyes and light goes in,
I shall be eating a traveller's heavy meal
Made much of by the kitchen staff. Our house
Is not a tabernacle, miracles are forgotten
In usefulness, the weight and irony of love.

PENGUIN MODERN POETS

Your Attention Please

The Polar DEW has just warned that
A nuclear rocket strike of
At least one thousand megatons
Has been launched by the enemy
Directly at our major cities.
This announcement will take
Two and a quarter minutes to make,
You therefore have a further
Eight and a quarter minutes
To comply with the shelter
Requirements published in the Civil
Defence Code – section Atomic Attack.
A specially shortened Mass
Will be broadcast at the end
Of this announcement –
Protestant and Jewish services
Will begin simultaneously –
Select your wavelength immediately
According to instructions
In the Defence Code. Do not
Take well-loved pets (including birds)
Into your shelter – they will consume
Fresh air. Leave the old and bed-
ridden, you can do nothing for them.
Remember to press the sealing
Switch when everyone is in
The shelter. Set the radiation
Aerial, turn on the geiger barometer.
Turn off your television now.

Turn off your radio immediately
The Services end. At the same time
Secure explosion plugs in the ears
Of each member of your family. Take
Down your plasma flasks. Give your children
The pills marked one and two
In the C.D. green container, then put
Them to bed. Do not break
The inside airlock seals until
The radiation All Clear shows
(Watch for the cuckoo in your
perspex panel), or your District
Touring Doctor rings your bell.
If before this, your air becomes
Exhausted or if any of your family
Is critically injured, administer
The capsules marked 'Valley Forge'
(Red pocket in No. 1 Survival Kit)
For painless death. (Catholics
Will have been instructed by their priests
What to do in this eventuality.)
This announcement is ending. Our President
Has already given orders for
Massive retaliation – it will be
Decisive. Some of us may die.
Remember, statistically
It is not likely to be you.
All flags are flying fully dressed
On Government buildings – the sun is shining

Death is the least we have to fear.
We are all in the hands of God,
Whatever happens happens by His Will.
Now go quickly to your shelters.

Soliloquy at Potsdam

There are always the poor –
Getting themselves born in crowded houses,
Feeding on the parish, losing their teeth early
And learning to dodge blows, getting
Strong bodies – cases for the warped nut of the mind.
The masterful cat-o'-nine-tails, the merciful
Discipline of the hours of drill – better
Than being poor in crowded Europe, the swan-swept
Waters where the faces dredge for bread
And the soggy dead are robbed on their way to the grave.
I can hear it from this window, the musket-drill
On the barrack square. Later today I'll visit
The punishment block. Who else in Europe
Could take these verminous, clutching creatures
And break them into men? What of the shredded back
And the broken pelvis, when the side-drum sounds,
When the uniformed wave tilts and overwhelms
The cheese-trading burghers' world, the aldermanic
Principalities. The reformers sit at my table,
They talk well but they've never seen a battle
Or watched the formed brain in the flogged body
Marching to death on a bellyful of soup and orders.
There has to be misery so there can be discipline.
People will have to die because I cannot bear
Their clinging to life. Why are the best trumpeters
Always French? Watch the west, the watershed
Of revolution. Now back to Quantz. I like to think
That in an afternoon of three sonatas
A hundred regiments have marched more miles

Than lie between here and Vienna and not once
Has a man broken step. Who would be loved
If he could be feared and hated, yet still
Enjoy his lust, eat well and play the flute?

Nine o'Clock Thoughts on the 73 Bus

Client meeting at twelve, that lot of layabouts
Will have to be spoken up for, must tell Ann
To get a new ivy for the office, louts
I saw trying to touch her up, lovely bum
Though. Everyone tries to get as much sex as he can,
The copywriter is flushed by the client's sun.

Ghosts

1

A large woman in a kimono, her flesh
Already sweating in the poulticing heat
Of afternoon – just from her bath, she stands,
Propping her foot on a chair of faded pink,
Preparing to cut her corns. The sun
Simmers through the pimply glass – as if
Inside a light bulb, the room is lit with heat.
The window is the sun's lens, its dusty slice
Of light falls on the woman's foot. The woman
Is my Mother – the clicking of her scissors
Fascinates the little feminine boy
In striped shirt, Tootal tie, thick woollen socks,
His garters down. Memory insists the boy is me.
The house still stands where we stood then.
The inheritance I had, her only child,
Was her party melancholy and a body
Thickening like hers, the wide-pored flesh
Death broke into twenty years ago.

2

The red wind carrying dust on to my Sunday shoes
Reddens also my nostrils and my mouth.
I stand by the school's venerable, fifty-years-old,
Washed cement veranda, waiting for my Father.
The Bunya pines along the straggling drive
Drop chunky cones on gravel – windswept bees
Slog across the Masters' Garden to lemon flowers;

Boys shout, dogs bark, no second is quite silent.
My Father with the Headmaster comes to me.
It is Sunday, Parents' Visiting Day. The drive
Is churned by cars. When we go down town,
Despite milk shakes and a demure high tea
In the Canberra Temperance Hotel, I only sulk.
I have kept this priggishness, Father;
The smart world laps you round. Your fear of this
Small child is now my fear – my boarding-school
World of rules rules me – my ghost
Has caught me up to sit and judge
The nightmares that I have, memories of love.

3

My Mother married all that there was left
Of an Old Colonial Family. The money gone,
The family house remained, surrounded by the dogs
He'd buried, forty years a bachelor –
We came there every Sunday in a silver tram
For tennis, when my Mother was alive.
Sometimes I try to find my face in theirs:
My Father in the Lacrosse team, my Mother
Nursing in the War – they tell no story
In family photographs. Their city is changed;
Coca-cola bottles bounce upon their lawn,
No one grows flowers, picnics are no fun,
Their aviaries are full of shop-bought birds.
Who goes for weekends down the Bay
In thirty footers to St Helena, Peel and Jumpin' Pin?

No yachts stand off the Old People's Home,
Out past the crab-pot buoys and floating mangrove fruit.

I was born late in a late marriage. Psychiatrists
Say it makes no difference – but now I think
Of what was never said in a tropical house
Of five miscarriages. If the words were said
They'd start the deaths up that I left for dead.

Eat Early Earthapples

There were boys at my Prep. School my own age
And three stone heavier, who made fifty pounds
Over the holidays selling kangaroo hides
They'd skinned and pegged out themselves
On their fathers' stations. Many shaved, several
Slept with the maids – one I remember
Running his hand up the Irish maid's leg
At breakfast not ten feet away
From the Headmaster's enormous armature of head.
Then there were those marathon journeys home
In the train for the holidays, without sleepers,
And the carriages full of Glennie and Fairholme
Girls sitting up all night – some crying
In the lavatory, some sipping sweet sherry
From dark label-less bottles passed them in the dark,
Some knowing what to do and spattered
By Queensland Railways' coal dust trying
To do it on the floor, their black lisle
Stockings changed for wartime rayon. There were
So many ways of losing a troublesome innocence
But so many ways of keeping it too. Being troubled,
I found a sophistication which drove me mad
Sitting out dances, a viewed humiliation,
Walking through waltzes on boracic'd floors,
(Chopped horsehair rising, said to make girls sexy).
The girls were nicer than I needed, the Headmaster
Led the Jolly Miller, the knowing athletes
Waited for the Gypsy Tap, their stories next day
Full of what they'd managed on the dark verandah.

My schooldays when I was so eagerly unhappy
Have me back among them when I sleep
Freely associating with those baffled fears.
The lascivious miler, the confident three-quarter
Are thick men now with kids and problems.
There is no way back into their wormy Eden,
Ripe with girls, esplanaded with sex,
To stuff myself to sickness and forget
(Taking their chances, my old wounds averted)
The boy with something wrong reading a book
While the smut-skeined train goes homeward
Carrying the practised to the sensual city.

Reading MND in Form 4B

Miss Manning rules us middle-class children
Whose fathers can't afford the better schools
With blue, small, crow-tracked, cruel eyes.
Philomel with melody – a refrain
Summoning the nightingale, the brown bird
Which bruits the Northern Hemisphere with bells –
It could not live a summer in this heat.

Queen Titania, unaware of Oberon,
Is sleeping on a bank. Her fairy watch
Sings over her a lullaby,
The warm snakes hatch out in her dream.
Miss Manning is too fat for love,
We cannot imagine her like Miss Holden
Booking for weekends at the seaside
With officers on leave. This is not Athens
Or the woods of Warwickshire,
Lordly the democratic sun
Rides the gross and southerly glass.
Miss Manning sets the homework. Thirty boys
Leave the bard to tire on his morning wing;
Out on their asphalt the teams for Saturday
Wait, annunciations in purple ink,
Torments in locker rooms, nothing to hope for
But sleep, the reasonable view of magic.
We do not understand Shakespearean objects
Who must work and play: that gold stems from the sky:
It poisons 1944. To be young is to be in Hell,

Miss Manning will insulate us from this genius,
Rock the ground whereon these sleepers be.

Elsewhere there is war, here
It is early in an old morning, there is pollen
In the air, eucalyptus slipping past
The chalk and dusters – new feelings
In the oldest continent, a northern race
Living in the south. It is late indeed:
Jack shall have Jill, all shall be well,
Long past long standing eternity,
Eastern Standard Time.

POEMS ANCIENT AND MODERN

Vienna

This Imperial city
Needs no Empire: turks, saints, huge nineteenth-
Century geniuses,

Poets with the tic, the spade
Bearded patriarch who raised to the nth.
The power of love, these came

Here like spokes to their axle.
Europe needed a capital – tenth
Sons needed to be Civil

Servants: such imagined strength
Focused on a style. The statued squares
Don't know that wet Hungary

Isn't theirs. Their birds can fly
To Balaton. The attic's story
Is that Haydn was beaten

There. An old lady who liked
Hitler's voice says Schubert's family
Lived fourteen to a room. Now

The tall Minnesotan will
Tell his wife 'we wash too much, you can't be
A genius in America'.

At Whitsun cars and buses
Carry large dragonflies, God can fly
In this architecture. Dreams

Adorned like cream cakes fatten
The citizens; they wake to abuses
That need icing. Smiling men

Arrive at work at seven
a.m. and a tourist confesses
To his unknown neighbour he

Was unfaithful on the boat.
Grapes grow up to the tram terminuses,
Nature is one of the boasts

Of lost prestige. History
Which puts the pop singer and the iron-
haired conductor in the same

Plane crash has kept this city
To vindicate its geniuses.
The trivial is immortal.

Sydney Cove, 1788

The Governor loves to go mapping – round and round
The inlets of the Harbour in his pinnace.
He fingers a tree-fern, sniffs the ground

And hymns it with a unison of feet –
We march to church and executions. No one,
Even Banks, could match the flora of our fleet.

Grog from Madeira reminds us most of home,
More than the pork and British weevils do.
On a diet of flour, your hair comes out in your comb.

A seaman who tried to lie with a native girl
Ran off when he smelt her fatty hide.
Some say these oysters are the sort for pearls.

Green shoots of the Governor's wheat have browned.
A box of bibles was washed up today,
The chaplain gave them to two Methodists. Ross found

A convict selling a baby for a jug of rum.
Those black hills which wrestle with
The rain are called Blue Mountains. Come

Genocide or Jesus we can't work this land.
The sun has framed it for our moralists
To dry the bones of forgers in the sand.

We wake in the oven of its cloudless sky,
Already the blood-encircled sun is up.
Mad sharks swim in the convenient sea.

The Governor says we mustn't land a man
Or woman with gonorrhoea. Sound felons only
May leave their bodies in a hangman's land.

Where all is novel, the only rule's explore.
Amelia Levy and Elizabeth Fowles spent the night
With Corporal Plowman and Corporal Winxstead for

A shirt apiece. These are our home concerns.
The cantor curlew sings the surf asleep.
The moon inducts the lovers in the ferns.

Madame de Merteuil on 'The Loss of an Eye'

No letters. What's to become of an
Epistolary style it was no
Vanity to pride oneself on: chess
With a stupid curé, giving bad
Advice about abortions to girls
With long chins whom no vice could ruin
Nor uxoriousness ever spoil.
Delphine has two kittens – how can I
Wheedle the cook's son to set his humpbacked
Tom on them? The tom is almost blind. We're two
Cerberus surveyors of the dark.
A young man called today. I recognized
The smell of boredom, the trap closing
In his eyes, a provincial appetite
For fame – the foxy diarist of love
Just waiting for old age to wax the world's
Ears with sententious aphorisms.
Sitting before a moral dish of nectarines,
I am pregnant again with self-love.
Crippled, sun stickying the socket
Of my dead eye, I choose *work*.
I can still plot the overthrow
Of a seminarist (a cut-price
Pascal with warts), plan the humbling of
A local Sévigné, wait calmly
For death to pay the courtesy of a call,
An old woman smelling lilac while her
Functionaries do evil in the sun.

The World of Simon Raven

Rooks are raging where great elms were felled,
Family silver's been lent for the Fête,
Nanny's facing Nigel with stained sheets,
Telegrams announce James is expelled,
Mrs Diamond from Sea View Estate
Tempts a team in training with boiled sweets.

Meanwhile sturgeon from Odessa packed
For Black's and Tan's, renowned St James's Clubs,
Laced with spanish fly, cause randy scenes
At Ascot, a Bishop's face is smacked;
Debs and guardsmen break up Chelsea pubs,
Blackmailers send snaps to dons at Queen's.

Unpaid Mess Bills get a Blue cashiered,
Boys from Balham pelt a First in Greats
With Latin Grammars, Israeli agents
Put pubic lice in Prince Muhammad's beard,
Doctor Boyce cuts off his cousin Kate's
Clitoris – the favourite fails the fence,

Bookies' reminders frighten Adjutants,
Crockford's man is found with a marked deck.
Somewhere beyond Maidenhead an old
Lady rings her bank for an advance
On her pension, sends her son a cheque,
Watches with the cat as it gets cold.

Homage to Gaetano Donizetti

There was a sugar farmer's son (hyperthyroid)
I knew who was just like Nemorino,
And a girl in the Everest Milk Bar
Whose tits rubbed the cold of the ice-cream churn
As she reached down with her cheating scoop –
You saw more if you asked for strawberry –
She had a cold Christ hung over that defile
Crucified in silver, his apotheosis
In dry ice fumes. She was just like bel'Adina,
All the magic in the world wouldn't get
Your hand down her front unless she'd heard
Your rich uncle had just died.
Transistors behind her played Pat Boone,
But only to make a money music
In the till. Dear Master, what they say
About your big guitar is academic prejudice.
The truth is Dr Dulcamara's got
The Times Music Critic's job; the rustici
Are cooking on Sicilian gas, Venetian composers
Are setting Goethe to gongs and spiels and phones,
Teutons still come south to add a little
Cantilena to their klangschönheit
(Not to mention the boys of Naples), and those apostles,
The Twelve Notes, are at work on their Acts
To beautify our arrogance. Why should you care
That your audience are stuffed shirts if you know
That half at least have paid up for their seats.

The Great Poet Comes Here in Winter

Frau Antonia is a cabbage:
If I were a grub I'd eat a hole in her.
Here they deliver the milk up a private path
Slippery as spit – her goddess' hands
Turn it to milk puddings. Blow, little wind,
Steer in off this cardboard sea,
You are acclimatized like these vines
Warring on an inch of topsoil
You are agent of the Golden Republic,
So still blow for me – our flowers look one way,
If I were a good poet I would walk on the sea.

The sea is actually made of eyes.
Whether of drowned fishermen or of peasants
Accustomed to the hard bargains of the saints
I cannot say. Whether there will be
Any mail from Paris or even broccoli
For dinner is in doubt. My hat blew off the planet,
I knelt by the infinite sand of the stars
And prayed for all men. Being German, I have a lot of soul.
Nevertheless, why am I crying in this garden?
I refuse to die till fashion comes back to spats.
From this turret the Adriatic
Burns down the galley lanes to starved Ragusa,
How strange it can wash up condoms.
The world is coming unstitched at the seams.
All yesterday the weather was a taste
In my mouth, I saw the notes of Beethoven
Lying on the ground, from the horn

Of a gramophone I heard Crivelli's cucumbers
Crying out for paint. In the eyes of a stray bitch
Ribbed with hunger, heavy with young,
I saw the peneplain of all imagined
Misery, horizontal and wider than the world.
I gave her my unwrapped sugar. We said Mass
Together, she licking my fingers and me
Knowing how she would die, not glad to have lived.
She took her need away, I thought her selfish
But stronger than God and more beautiful company.

Encounter in Antioch

Your God became a man, our grandest men
Have trouble becoming Gods. You've got
Three Legions now and their influence grows
With the superstition of the Emperor.
And those terrible Alexandrian disputers
Always wanting to cut their balls off
And everybody else's too. No wonder
Three-headed goats are coming out of
The desert. I met a man had three shits
A day in honour of the Trinity.
But one day this theologian's world
Of pain and dirt may surprise you,
The wind off the sea may bring the Tyrian
Scent to your garden, and then you hear
A million brainless jaws jarring the lawn,
You're fanned by a million ledger leaves
Turned by quilted, careful hands.
Drink down a cup of water and look out
On the town – the someone whose hat
You laugh at may stop and the great tide start
To come in on his stranger's gifted face.

A PORTER FOLIO

The Last of the Dinosaurs

Chalky, you've gone –
the only one to see the last
stegosaurus, the blue-edged plain
with bald egg-eaters blurring it,
eighty days' rain
before the mating season
and parsley blades neck high –

nice to have known such niceness,
these Cretaceous days!
Tyranno – sore arse – Rex
and other thick necks
thrive. Where's the gentle
ninety ton nonsense
we ate mustard grass beside?

So much time and blue.
That great arc telling
the centuries with its pivotless
movement, tick, tock, tick:
you can watch evolution
in those hairy faces
and poor Protoceratops being sick.

Another gentle day and
nothing to do. When you've lasted
150 million years
you can stand the sound of time.
Some day a mind is going to come

and question all this dance –
I've left footprints in the sand.

Valete and Salvete.
I hear the wintering waters rise
under the hemstitched sky.
Put me in the anthologies,
darling, like Horace almost
killed by a falling tree;
life is a dream or very nearly.

My Late T'ang Phase

Unexpected sun on white icing terraces,
Little girls ringing my doorbell and giggling,
More than a lifetime between six o'clock and seven,
Enough loneliness for a novel, enough poise.
Ambition fights talent more than sloth does.
I sit in the warmer, the caramel darkness
Watching two worldly eyes: where is the inseminate
Of boredom, the Rilke of the inflamed will?

Why be beleaguered by nerves only?
Why not have tanned historical enemies?
My friends find new forms which make kites
Of confessions: whatever your taste there's
Blood here to back it. I take eight-hundred page
Histories of Florence from Paddington Library.
I know nine tabby cats, all pregnant. News?
They dug up the dead who were smiling.

Fantasia on a Line of Stefan George

I shall die if I do not touch your body.
If I cannot claim a small priest-like
Privilege at your waist, my masks
Of face will slip, no tides will work
Your body's shores, no storms rouse
That inland sea. On a hectoring day
I stood in the Natural History Museum
And couldn't breathe. The blue whale
And the passenger pigeon worried for me,
Surely my fingers were losing their prints,
I had no history in my bones, I was
Transparent as a finished gesture.
Where you are is life: this sunlessness
Is only inside my head,
The inverse paradise, rain forest where
Evolution's mother blocked with eggs
Waddles with beak aloft to spin
The thread of fear that leads back to you.

A Hoplite's Helmet

Inside this helmet
A brain known to great brains

Moved to kill,
The object was in the orders.

The helmetless lover
And boozer fathered as many

New skulls as any,
But he put the helmet back on. You can

Frighten the cat
Poking your fingers through the eye pieces.

When death's eyes
Make a play for me let him approach

In this helmet;
It's sat on some howling scenes –

Witness the old lady
Of Corinth who couldn't be parted

From her sponges;
A yellow bean drying – that was a chunk

Of Epaminondas's brain,
You meet the greatest people in battle.

The helmet's worth
A thousand pounds. Verdigris takes

A month to form
And lasts two thousand years. As many

Million dead
Must come again before this metal dies.

Seahorses

When we were children
We would cheer to find a seahorse
Among the wrack the breakers lifted
On to the beach. Sometimes two or three were together,
A team to pull a chariot of cuttle,
Or like a suicide wreathed in fine
Sea ivy and bleached sea roses
One stiff but apologetic in its trance.
Seahorses were vikings;
Somewhere they impassively
Launched on garrulous currents
Seeking a far grave: wherever
That was, they set their stallion
Noses to it, ready to be garnered
In the sea's time at the sea's pleasure.
If we wondered why we loved them
We might have thought
They were the only creatures which had to die
Before we could see them –
In this early rule of death we'd recognize
The armorial pride of head, the unbending
Seriousness of small creatures,
Credit them with the sea's rare love
Which threw them to us in their beauty,
Unlike the vast and pitiable whale
Which must be quickly buried for its smell.

Futurity

If you could guess at seven
That the little girl with plaits
And the band on her teeth would be
Fata Morgana the great star and Alice
The most invited girl in the street
Would later turn her feast of eyes
On the recurring chianti bottles
Of the asylum wallpaper
Counting forever up to ten
With no crack in the world to follow,
If Sophonisba with the spots
Playing Czerny in the sun
Through afternoons of talc and zinnias
Could guess to what use a half-moon
Carving knife might be put,
If Ralph the even-tempered Saxon
Who carried his bat through ten
Summers could prognosticate
His two children and the pulp
He'd make of their brains with a new
Tack hammer – if all these could
Then perhaps you could have seen
Standing beside the mossy overflow
Of the rain tank that your nerves'
Carnival would sink to a smile
From Bridget, to three children
And a clock of dead chimes, that and
A three inch par in the local paper
When you saved an oiled seagull

From the Council boatshed, crying
And smiling for one death the less,
This strange fate of a tropical Nietzsche
Condemned to the Bizet of his dreams,
A silted sinus and two doctors
Casting short shadows on the lawn.

The History of Music from 'Three Poems for Music'

Though this is not in Hesiod,
Music was stolen from a God:

Not fire but notes the primal giver
Paid for with helpings of his liver

And virtuosi of the earth
Outsang the Gods who gave them birth.

When Orpheus plays we meet Apollo,
When there's theology to swallow

We set it to music, our greatest art,
One that's both intellect *and* heart,

There war and peace alike depict us
(Drums and trumpets in the Benedictus) –

It sang beneath the Grecian boat,
It kept Pythagoras afloat,

It suffered poets, critics, chat
And will no doubt survive Darmstadt;

This brandy of the damned of course
To some is just a bottled sauce,

Its treasons, spoils and stratagems
Aleatory as women's hems

Yet beauty who indulged the swan
At death completes her with a song

And Paradise till we are there
Is in these measured lengths of air.

Fair Go for Anglo-Saxons

(A near-contemporary gallimaufry)

1 Provincial Messiah

To be under thirty
and already have written ten pronunciamenti,
to think all older writers
only want to lay you
and boast of the girls you've laid,
to think no one is any good
except a poet from Alberta,
Catullus and some friends
who run a mimeographed magazine,
to misquote Ovid, misrepresent Pound,
misunderstand Olson and never
have heard of Edwin Arlington Robinson,
to have to print your girl friend's
things alongside your own,

to be all this is better
than to have talent and have to write well.

2 At the Trat'

The translator of aphorisms
is wining and dining the actress/playwright/
wife of the famous TV Producer.
Everyone in the restaurant, including
the determined client-suitors,
is eavesdropping now. Red wine
and vintage sex life spill among

Sicilian smiles. She's an old hand –
she can stick to Lichtenberg
and the hundred German devils
while he gets a feel in.
The waiters are sending money home.
Now says Old Ruby Nose topping up his glass
the goat-faced youth are knocking up the girls
in the randy grass of Agrigentum.
In her next play she retells the story
of Persephone: we winter with her
as she greets the God in jeans.

3 Sibylline Stutterings

After the New Emancipation
The New Rudeness,
After the New Heterosexuality
The New Cruelty,
After the New Live Art
The New Messiahs,
After the New Violence
The New Dandyism,
After the New Controversy
The New In-Touchness,
After the New Complexity
The New Indeterminacy,
After the New Toughness
The New Lyricism,

After the New Expressionism
The New Communication,
After the New Concern
The New Loneliness.

4 Lines

She's loyal to the marmalade she bought in Danzig
They found paddi-pads in the Chairman's trunks
Boethius or Bride to the Thing in the Box: two good reads
Wise old eyes have perused the small print
He told her he didn't love her in the Restful Tray
Proof of genius: fatty degeneration of the heart
She was buried holding her Tolkien books
Sunday and the fish are parsing the reviews
O for Pauline in the french nylon knickers
So neighbourly, a candid Canuck and a smiling Finn
God died underfoot – in the steps of the master
Köchel, even the fifth edition notwithstanding, the score
includes bassoons
The comic novelists' convention is ending

5 Twenty-four lines

A common cold wins
provinces for a man,
an arbiter of elegance
rides into town on a Bactrian camel

The ravines of this city
are full of gold and milkshakes:
a light box where the pain shows up,
I mean the world, our clean small world

Face to face with wise Inquisitors
I tore my skin in night despair,
I am the Quinbus Flestrin
of this louche Lilliput

A lot of religious black men
strip the air of its European clothes,
the occupying army leaves behind
a complete set of the Waverley Novels

Can you solve the problem
of the Pervigilium Veneris
or graft the Peace Rose
on the Lady Buchanan?

The forks are shut up in the drawer,
the word has come among us –
I that in health was and . . .
wounds healed forever leave a scar.

6 Half-Mast Poems

The quick brown fox jumped over
        the lazy dog. The MFH
had been up typing all night.

Open the window and let it in
        said the parson. I want a terror
applicable to my Sunday sermon.

Oxford Marmalade is American owned.
        Ten public-spirited Coopers
resign from the Telephone Directory.

The pollen count in London was 107.
        That was the day he caught the Speaker's eye
In the Westminster Public Convenience.

Now for the great work, begun among the ruins
        of Western Civilization, the start of the long return,
this morning in the ABC in Westbourne Grove . . .

Two Nations!
The Rich and the Poor, the South and the North?
No, the Attractive and the Unattractive.

The Porter Song Book

1 Wir haben beide lange Zeit geschwiegen

We sit untalkative in a room
The light is leaving: after such words
The flesh cannot get close enough
To hold half-smiles. Love's angel
Will not come; the warm world
Of lime trees, madness and
Pianoforte albums has given way
To goadings in the yellow gloom
Of Gospel Oak. The silence after love
Is broken, not by the closing wings
Of the Nineteenth Century, but by
An article on topless dresses
Tossed into stale air. This severity
Is just to vex. From the fenced wood
A black spirit flaps up to our eaves.

2 Story from a Travel Book

They spent three months in the marshes.
Love and the water turned them into
Beautiful animals. They told their rescuers
The wide Delta sun steamed up
Like a river boat, each of them became
A soothsayer, sounds of struck brass
Were lost in the flattened reeds.
There was one death – baked in golden mud
He lay among a childish people
Caressed by keening. One great soul

Saw the light go out, reached for
The Akkadian dark: smelling a little of urine,
He was taking one step on to the stars
When a French engineer found him,
Blue-eyed, still recognizably European,
But suffering from malnutrition that
No river dog or girl of twelve
Could be companion to or compensate.

4 Clairvoyant

You've narrowed the horizon to a noose
And in anxiety bang about the house,
The enemy of vases. One or two people,
Your husband for a start, will die
When eventually they get past you
To the disneyland inside your head.
You're a spiky girl the children love,
You always settle with the milkman early;
But still you gaze through lines and dream
Of living: here is peace, the reach
Of an old river with lawns to its edge
And an opposite bank nobody has seen.

6 Genius Loci

        Look, nothing has changed –
the great spoor have never faded,
the jugular tips blood from a new quarry,
        there is a parting by an iron fountain,
rays of water fan from the sun of this place

and there in his accustomed corner
sits nature's godson,
nursing his face on the water's skin.
Do not come, love, if you are afraid
to turn into a barbered shrub:
what we are now the fire will hold.

11 Poetry

An old art spreading rumours about
Paradise, it begs outside the gates
Of the gods: the active gods come out.

14 From an Old Master

On the green cloth of summer lie
Bullrushes, water, ducks and sky.
There Christ, a sinless silver boy,
In his mother's lap sits like a toy;
A sapling lapped in pale green moss
Casts down the shadow of the Cross.

THE LAST OF ENGLAND

The Last of England

It's quiet here among the haunted tenses:
Dread Swiss germs pass the rabbit's throat,
Chemical rain in its brave green hat
Drinks at a South Coast Bar, the hedgehog
Preens on nylon, we dance in Tyrolean
Drag whose mothers were McGregors,
Exiled seas fill every cubit of the bay.

Sailing away from ourselves, we feel
The gentle tug of water at the quay –
Language of the liberal dead speaks
From the soil of Highgate, tears
Show a great water table is intact.
You cannot leave England, it turns
A planet majestically in the mind.

A Meredithian Treatment

We knew at the time that he was dangerous,
I for one had an instinctive loathing –
The dirt, the bells, the glasses tied with string –
Yet we thought of this as something wrong with us.
The past is dead, the future dead, the now
Is here, an apotheosis of girls begins.
He who takes nothing stronger than aspirins
Leads us in worship of the Dulcet Cow,
A sociologist issues us with parts!
I am King Pentheus, I shall sort out Thebes;
It's not the queers and chewers of poppy seeds
I hate, it's that gammony gang of tarts
That's bringing normal sex into disrepute;
They've read the legend wrong, my mother's torn
Me apart already, now I am reborn
In huge respectability, with a gun in my suit.

Short Story

Maureen makes a rope and ribbon model
of Nicholas, plaiting him a big member,
then puts it on to cook.

Her stove is patented 'The White Goddess'.

Nick is, as the novelists say,
an ordinary, young, good-looking,
empty, ambitious, self-fascinated shit.

I think we'll give Maureen
a weekly Group Analysis session.

Dr Brandeis is away at a conference,
what is she going to do?

Puts sixty-seven barbiturates in a tumbler
just to look at them.

Nick's saying to Mr Ballantine,
'terrific, I'm screwing this bird
and her bloody dog comes up and licks my balls.'

Maureen enters a dream,
a pride of lions walks from the upturned glass –
over their prophetic thighs
puffs the angel of death.

'If she had to go for pills why couldn't
she make it *the* Pill.'

The lions are in front of plexiglas
sunning in the architect's patio,
noiselessly they cross the nursing home
and sip her quiet milk.

The Samaritans send her Norman O. Brown.

She could become an assistant
with Abacus:
no, I'll set her up cataloguing
maiolica in a private collection.

I'm going to give Nick
a mild dose, but I can't stop him
becoming Brand Manager.

I'm wearing God's shirt.

We'll leave Maureen under the departure board
at Waterloo looking up a train to Godalming.

The trouble is you can't write about dreams.

What was caught in Surrey in the headlights?

This all came about because I had
a strong letter asking me
why not write a poem where the woman
is the despised and loving creature
for a change.

Diana and Actaeon

You only think you see them
the dolorous dogs of conscience

You hear only yourself
to have looked at the naked moon

The moon rises again
under the quicks of your nails

That is the moon's music
from the far side of a syringe

They are her officers
the moon team under Doctor Lucubrare

Soon she will come to see you
she has her times of the month

And memories. Memories of the sun
things not looked at directly

You looked and fancied and she knew
now there is no safety anywhere

She gives flowers to a nurse
for certain she has seen your grave

From the bottom of the lift-well
the howls of the baskervilles

The Workers

The people of the meniscus
see over the edge of the world

Valerie runs her hand along Hugues' bright creases
and takes her finger within an inch
of his sleeping penis in Independence Square,
she loves him over coffee and pigeons
and over the complications of her doubt

It takes a whole Black Country
and at least one new oxidizing process
to maintain the canals in her fallen eyelids

Justice of the sun, she says, on the water –
this was once the capital of the wool trade
when the bankers were the nouveaux riches –
calm of the duck-billed dawn
and the cerise and cerulean pills!

Their planes are honed on the sky
and they are together beside the *Geertgen tot Sint Jans*,
a torturer's and a peasant's descendants

On the broad back of money
are the fine moles of sensibility –
she reads that in a novel
and thinks how like a girl in a novel
she is –
          she knows how to
find a switch and turn the room

to a D Major landscape
          she has a vision
that all the rest are in the mines
where the D Major is dug,
the peruked miners,
workers at the star-hot centre
filling the hoppers with life
and she and her lover at the end
of the beautiful cables, fed and balanced
and warmed, thinning down, rarefied
and soon to have wings –
the libraries and the switches and the slurry
are programmed for this,
her delicacy and radiant quickness,
her crystalline migraine which they like ants
are the distant and decent makers of

A Consumer's Report

The name of the product I tested is *Life*,
I have completed the form you sent me
and understand that my answers are confidential.

I had it as a gift,
I didn't feel much while using it,
in fact I think I'd have liked to be more excited.
It seemed gentle on the hands
but left an embarrassing deposit behind.
It was not economical
and I have used much more than I thought
(I suppose I have about half left
but it's difficult to tell) –
although the instructions are fairly large
there are so many of them
I don't know which to follow, especially
as they seem to contradict each other.
I'm not sure such a thing
should be put in the way of children –
It's difficult to think of a purpose
for it. One of my friends says
it's just to keep its maker in a job.
Also the price is much too high.
Things are piling up so fast,
after all, the world got by
for a thousand million years
without this, do we need it now?
(Incidentally, please ask your man
to stop calling me 'the respondent',

I don't like the sound of it.)
There seems to be a lot of different labels,
sizes and colours should be uniform,
the shape is awkward, it's waterproof
but not heat resistant, it doesn't keep
yet it's very difficult to get rid of:
whenever they make it cheaper they seem
to put less in – if you say you don't
want it, then it's delivered anyway.
I'd agree it's a popular product,
it's got into the language; people
even say they're on the side of it.
Personally I think it's overdone,
a small thing people are ready
to behave badly about. I think
we should take it for granted. If its
experts are called philosophers or market
researchers or historians, we shouldn't
care. We are the consumers and the last
law makers. So finally, I'd buy it.
But the question of a 'best buy'
I'd like to leave until I get
the competitive product you said you'd send.

Stroking the Chin*

Some possibilities

At the same time
emit a thin bat sound,
sitting in the William Morris chair
looking at the Scandinavian blind,
the easiest way into the mountains
and the land of monkey tails.

Things don't happen this way,
I write them down this way
and I pull from my chin
two hairs I've allowed to grow –
so much for historicism, I say.

Remembering her sentimentally,
feel to see if I've shaved,
for she wasn't always good-tempered,
being a good fuck but a spiky human being.

If I centre my thumb
in the almost non-existent
dimple of my chin and touch
my four reachable moles
with my four free fingers
        that brunette

* Spelt *Ch'in*, this is a Chinese lute. There are a number of acknowledged ways of playing it, each descriptive of a mood or state of mind. They are called Ways of Stroking the *Ch'in*.

will leave her publisher
and cross the tiled floor
of the restaurant to invite
me back to Montagu Square
for the afternoon.

In the Lord High Admiral's style,
the other arm leaning on an astrolabe,
elbow on Mandeville and Marco Polo,
watch them bring aboard three trussed Indians,
some dull gold in a nest
of parrot feathers and a vein
of pox for the sake of history –
the belief in progress is worth it.

Caught between the smell of celery
and the sun's incandescence
on the polished back of a brush
pinch dry flesh at mean temperature,
my agreeable dewlap,
and curl up like a Degas print.

After the oven exploded
I passed for black
and wrote three articles
for liberal journals
and occasioned
a season of old
Eddie Cantor films –
my statue, chin in hand,

is to be erected
in a small South London park
to illustrate the First
Mode of Opportunity.
Two severed heads
with trailing beards
look out of a
Nineties photograph –
Chinoiserie!

Let Me Bore You with My Slides

It's this new colour process –
the world licks the back of our hands,
four of us on the winter sands
squinting at the soft-backed sea.

Brown for Hester in her aviatrix suit,
little girl in love with an iced lolly,
damson for Juliet and melancholy
sniffed and snapped at by the puppy waves.

And we two stand together on the wall
joined by the membrane of one life,
love's face peers between husband and wife,
a cautious colour like afternoon.

The Sadness of the Creatures

We live in a third-floor flat
among gentle predators
and our food comes often
frozen but in its own shape
(for we hate euphemisms
as you would expect) and our cat's
food comes in tins, other than
scraps of the real thing and she
like a clever cat makes milk
of it for her kittens: we shout
of course but it's electric
like those phantom storms
in the tropics and we think of
the neighbours – I'm not writing
this to say how guilty
we are like some well-paid
theologian at an American
College on a lake
or even to congratulate
the greedy kittens who have
found their mittens and are up
to their eyes in pie – I know
lots of ways of upsetting
God's syllogisms, real
seminar-shakers some of them,
but I'm an historical cat
and I run on rails and so
I don't frame those little poems
which take three lines to

get under your feet –
you know the kind of thing –
The water I boiled the lobster in
is cool enough to top
up the chrysanthemums.
No, I'm acquisitive and have
one hundred and seven Bach
Cantatas at the last count,
but these are things of the spirit
and my wife and our children
and I are animals (biologically
speaking) which is how the world
talks to us, moving on the billiard
table of green London, the sun's
red eye and the cat's green eye
focusing for an end. I know
and you know and we all know
that the certain end of each of us
could be the end of all of us,
but if you asked me what
frightened me most, I wouldn't
say the total bang or even
the circling clot in the red drains
but the picture of a lit room
where two people not disposed
to quarrel have met so
oblique a slant of the dark
they can find no words for
their appalled hurt but only

ride the rearing greyness:
there is convalescence from this,
jokes and love and reassurance,
but never enough and never
convincing and when the cats
come brushing for food their soft
aggression is hateful;
the trees rob the earth and the earth
sucks the rain and the children
burgeon in a time of invalids –
it seems a trio sonata
is playing from a bullock's
skull and the God of Man
is born in a tub of entrails;
all man's regret is no more
than Attila with a cold
and no Saviour here or
in Science Fiction will come
without a Massacre of the Innocents
and a Rape of El Dorado.

On This Day I Complete My Fortieth Year

Although art is autonomous
somebody has to live in the poet's body
and get the stuff out through his head,
          someone has to suffer

especially the boring sociology of it
and the boring history, the class war
and worst of all the matter of good luck,
          that is to say bad luck –

for in the end it is his fault, i.e. your fault
not to be born Lord Byron and saying
there has already been a Lord Byron is no excuse –
          he found it no excuse –

to have a weatherboard house and a white
paling fence and poinsettias and palm nuts
instead of Newstead Abbey and owls and graves
          and not even a club foot;

above all to miss the European gloom
in the endless eleven o'clock heat among
the lightweight suits and warped verandahs,
          an apprenticeship, not a pilgrimage –

the girl down the road vomiting dimity
incisored peanuts, the bristly boss speaking
with a captain's certainty to the clerk,
          'we run a neat ship here':

well, at forty, the grievances lie around
like terminal moraine and they mean
nothing unless you pay a man in Frognal
to categorize them for you

but there are two sorts of detritus, one a pile
of moon-ore, the workings of the astonished
mole who breathes through your journalism
'the air of another planet',

his silver castings are cherished in books and papers
and you're grateful for what he can grub up
though you know it's little enough beside
the sea of tranquillity –

the second sort is a catalogue of bitterness,
just samples of death and fat worlds of pain
that sail like airships through bed-sit posters
and never burst or deflate;

far more real than a screaming letter,
more embarrassing than an unopened statement
from the bank, more memorable than a small
dishonesty to a parent –

but to make a resolution will not help,
Greece needs liberating but not by me,
I am likely to find my Sapphics not verses
but ladies in Queensway,

so I am piling on fuel for the dark,
jamming the pilgrims on tubular chairs
while the NHS doctor checks my canals,
          my ports and my purlieus,

praying that the machine may work a while
longer, since I haven't programmed it
yet, suiting it to a divisive music
          that is the mind's swell

and which in my unchosen way
I marked out so many years ago
in the hot promises as a gift I must follow,
          'howling to my art'

as the master put it while he was still young –
these are the epiphanies of a poor light,
the ghosts of mid-channel, the banging doors
          of the state sirocco.

'The Sanitized Sonnets'

4

Much have I travelled in the realms of gold
for which I thank the Paddington and Westminster
Public Libraries: and I have never said sir
to anyone since I was seventeen years old.

I've wasted forty years thinking about
what to write on my gravestone. Here lies
five foot eleven, thirteen stone, brown eyes,
who got his tenses wrong and his zip caught.

He had a high temperature called mother
and knew the Köchel catalogue by heart,
he is the programmers' A. N. Other

but I in my first person present will
do my duty as a consumer of art –
Milton! Dryden! Shakespeare! Overkill!

PREACHING TO THE CONVERTED

The King of the Cats is Dead

The light on his thigh was like
a waterfall in Iceland, and his hair
was the tidal rip between two rocks,
his claws retracted sat in softness
deeper than the ancient moss of Blarney,
his claws extended were the coulter
of the gods and a raw March wind
was in his merely agricultural yawn.
Between his back legs was a catapult
of fecundity and he was riggish
as a red-haired man. The girls
of our nation felt him brush their legs
when they were bored with telling rosaries –
at night he clawed their brains in their
coffined beds and his walnut mind
wrinkled on their scalps. His holidays
were upside down in water and then
his face was like the sun: his smell
was in the peat smoke and even his midden
was a harmony of honey. When he stalked
his momentary mice the land shook
as though Atlantic waves were bowling
at the western walls. But his eyes
were the greatest thing about him.
They burned low and red so that drunks
saw them like two stars above a hedge,
they held the look of last eyes
in a drowning man, they were the sight
the rebel angels saw the first morning

of expulsion. And he is dead – a voice
from the centre of the earth told of his death
by treachery, that he lies in a hole
of infamy, his kidneys and his liver
torn from his body.

Therefore tell
the men and horses of the market-place,
the swallows laying twigs, the salmon
on the ladder that nothing is
as it has been

time is explored
and all is known, the portents
are of brief and brutal things, since
all must hear the words of desolation,
The King of the Cats is Dead

and it
is only Monday in the world.

Fossil Gathering

Armed with hammers, we move along the cliff
Whose blue wall keeps a million million deaths;
The surf is low, the heat haze screens the stiff-
Backed searchers for imprisoned crystals. Blind
Eyes of belemnites watch from narrow clefts,
Jurassic sun shines on them while they're mined.

The children look them up in paperbacks
And break an Ancient with impatient ease.
Sorted and cleaned, the fossils are in stacks,
Prepared and dressed for classrooms and jam jars –
At night in cupboards the reassembled seas
Break over England, straining for the stars.

A Little Guide in Colour tells us how
These creatures sank in their unconscious time,
That life in going leaves a husk the plough
Or amateur collector can displace,
That every feeling thing ascends from slime
To selfhood and in dying finds a face.

May, 1945

As the Allied tanks trod Germany to shard
and no man had seen a fresh-pressed uniform
for six months, as the fire storm
bit out the core of Dresden yard by yard,

as farmers hid turnips for the after-war,
as cadets going to die passed Waffen SS
tearing identifications from their battledress,
the Russians only three days from the Brandenburger Tor –

in the very hell of sticks and blood and brick dust
as Germany the phoenix burned, the wraith
of History pursed its lips and spoke, thus:

To go with teeth and toes and human soap,
the radio will broadcast Bruckner's Eighth
so that good and evil may die in equal hope.

Sex and the Over-Forties

It's too good for them,
they look so unattractive undressed –
let them read paperbacks!

A few things to keep in readiness –
a flensing knife, a ceiling mirror,
a cassette of *The Broken Heart*.

More luncheons than lust,
more meetings on Northern Line stations,
more discussions of children's careers.

A postcard from years back –
I'm twenty-one, in Italy and in love!
Wagner wrote *Tristan* at forty-four.

Trying it with noises and in strange positions,
trying it with the young themselves,
trying to keep it up with the Joneses!

All words and no play,
all animals fleeing a forest fire,
all Apollo's grafters running.

Back to the dream in the garden,
back to the pictures in the drawer,
back to back, tonight and every night.

Dream Restaurant

In this restaurant the flowers double-talk,
they have overheard our dates to die:
my side-plate is a schism of the moon.

Why is everybody leaving, elbowing aside
chafing dishes and napkin barbicans,
why has a nimbus ducked the world in blue?

These radical ends of thought: my liver
is excoriated from my back, I have hidden
my pain like valuables in a vase.

I must be firm on vulgar instances –
a bell ringing like spiteful rain at sea,
a photograph that bloodies my right hand.

Where we eat is the world, I didn't dream it:
my mouth is full of eucharist, forgive me
if I've swallowed the words for love.

They will come back, the pain comes back,
return of the native at dusk or dawn,
private, without flowers, sicking up his words.

Dark and dark, the inside of the dark.
I am the world's digestion, I am love,
I eat and am eaten perpetually.

In the Giving Vein

The evidence, like the weather, is from
An inner storm; the poem, like every poem,
Will be merely a beginning, the daring work
For Venus's mirror, a heap of ashes,
Never to be finished though complete:
The mirror must be walked through
And the one of many million crosses
Borne – the pollen cloud dispersing, spruce
Sadists and armorial villains stand
Plausibly among scales and trumpets,
Violence and punctilio masked by falling
Almond blossom; then from the dream
A voice proclaims the flag and day of evil,
Indifferent to irony and liberal shame.

This is the gift I would refuse – I'd take
Well-water from a town of towers,
Make history of grey femurs and hot
Processions watched from reedy rivers:
The ingredients are myself, a nuisance
In a marmalade tomb grinning at
Centuries of cards, a savant with
A Cockney grammar interrupted as
The aristocratic plane drops, a storm
Of poets landing like Columbus' men
To bring back a pox to infect the twenty-six
Letters of the alphabet. There'll be no home
But that low-water amniotic
Whose sounds are caucus to the will to live.

No pressure on my chest and yet I'm not
In the giving vein. I have about me
Those moveables of eyes that dreams
Have sanctified. The weather is dull, no mist,
The lake is flowing in the wrong direction,
Early to work and the postman with
Words that fall down if they're leaned on.
Extraordinary that victory can be snatched
From such small things – a shift in
The weight of nouns, a new nickname
For God, a flower lasting an extra day –
We're in a fire, singing; I'm the one
Whose voice you can't hear; perhaps my round
O is agony, I shall insist it's praise.

The Dust

How many divisions has the dust
as it drifts upon the lukewarm land?

We have matched it with our treaties,
our helicopter shadows;
when it shifts formation
there will be lights on after midnight
in several hexagonal rooms.

Plural, it plays with the calm of men.

The mortal magnolia has it like moth's wings,
it's shaken out as salt from a tablecloth.

The Two were formed from this,
according to instructions
in the Scout Book on that first of campings-out –
the cuscus looked and the slow worm sat
in a circle with itself: fasting, magnetism,
courage: they were our signs.

The Saviour of the State was accoutred
in his people's love, but a detachment of dust
rose from Spanish wheels.

Oh, but the dust, the gold-faced dust
from the Valley of Kings and Aunt Teresa's atomizer –
the aphids and the asteroids of change!

These are the priest's raised hands
and the lecturer's special slides
(for metropolitan audiences over thirty) –

As Doctor Danvers said – the cycle has one constant –
from the grub to the cyclone, the beta particle
to Donatello's chisel, the incorruptible body
to the pains of Hell –
only this milky dust.

Only dust the worm loved
singing at the river's mouth,
dust in the church of little spines,
dust where the library was burned.

Such clever men to start at starlight
when the dust lies low.

To know that when we land
the dust will be waiting.

Just as now a turn of wrist has sent a jot
of it over the rail to April.

Clear like a beast's old eyes
or Aphrodite's sweat-drops:

To please the dust by dying,
dying and returning –

To be worthy of the knowledge
that dust is only windows –

Not like the frightened Wit, brushing himself
ceaselessly behind sealed doors,

Nor the space in the crystal
where dust can never gather,

To live the while we live
just in this word, a dust.

Mort aux chats

There will be no more cats.
Cats spread infection,
cats pollute the air,
cats consume seven times
their own weight in food a week,
cats were worshipped in
decadent societies (Egypt
and Ancient Rome), the Greeks
had no use for cats. Cats
sit down to pee (our scientists
have proved it). The copulation
of cats is harrowing; they
are unbearably fond of the moon.
Perhaps they are all right in
their own country but their
traditions are alien to ours.
Cats smell, they can't help it,
you notice it going upstairs.
Cats watch too much television,
they can sleep through storms,
they stabbed us in the back
last time. There have never been
any great artists who were cats.
They don't deserve a capital C
except at the beginning of a sentence.
I blame my headache and my
plants dying on to cats.
Our district is full of them,
property values are falling.

When I dream of God I see
a Massacre of Cats. Why
should they insist on their own
language and religion, who
needs to purr to make his point?
Death to all cats! The Rule
of Dogs shall last a thousand years!

Tending towards the Condition

The news has reached the frogspawn,
our world is ransomed, spring rain
brings down a veil of weed, the Arno
the colour of Advocaat, another round
of tasks performed. To have nothing to say
fills large books with responsibilities –
as I said to the man in *Niccolino's*,
do away with form and you drown
in the infinite chances, especially
as darkness and other persons' phlegm
puts such a strain on you. As I sit,
slightly drunk with change from a thousand lire,
I hear the pens of cataloguers circling
the evening: in this episode the ghosts
of Hoboken and Pincherle remind me
how much time there is in sixty years.
I will put out sugar for the scholars
and steal their honey – a sort of happiness
is tombed in the *Volta dei Mercanti*,
a breeze springs up and fluffs the sparrows,
another half carafe sets the moon sailing
or a blaze of rain to cool the customers –
there is a shape to the world, more real
than time, more absolute than music.

Postcard Poems

Orcagna – Detail from the fresco, The Last Judgment, The Inferno – Santa Croce, Florence

Repentance comes too late. The camp fiends
put on a fashion show. Oh wring your hands
in eau-de-nil regret. Toasted with friends,
the damned tiptoe on the burning sands.
Orcagna, Florentine, your sexy smell
is semen frying in the pans of Hell.

Pisanello – La Principessa di Trebizonda – detail of fresco, Santa Anastasia, Verona

I have dreamed of green bishops
and almond-flavoured air,
I have seen devils hi-jack
the nimbus of a minor saint
from an Ossuary by an Inland Sea –
the Post is very bad, the wind
is making tourbillons around my hat,
it ruffles my cat Jesu, the four legs
of impassioned platitude;
from the depths of my calendar
I send you two words – MUCH LOVE!

J.M.W. Turner – The Parting of Hero and Leander – National Gallery, London

Love was always like this: a broken egg
in the sky, dawn with its regulation
heartbreak and evening with a train to catch.

The high buildings are not real, only the hopes.
Nous sommes aux mois d'amour.
Instead, the painter goes back in his eyes
and the poet dreams he sees this incredible sky.
Then the water breaks over his head. Praise
on your birthday from the swimmer and his gods.

Peter Phillips – Random Illusion No. 4 – Tate Gallery

Like the dove said, when you got
a military-industrial complex going
for you, you can blow rings round
any old abstract scruple and have
enough left over to endow the arts.
Big nations have wingspan and it ain't
Chrysler alone that mows down midgets.
Now all you liberal poets, get off
your blocks and come on hawkish!

Richard Hamilton – Interior II – Tate Gallery

The world is enormous, as the old
lens-grinder knew, inhaling fine
flour of death in his twilight room –
the home fleet of the past dresses
along my lifted arm and wherever
the archons shift their weight
a bruise of power shows. I am
becoming perfect in a room,
salvationist veal, nearer

the heart of truth, the wholly
responsive, appropriate number.

Pinturicchio – La Storia della Fortuna – Mosaic, Siena Cathedral

I cannot work out this allegory
of men and women on a crumbling cliff:
bare breasts with a sail, one foot on a globe
and one on a boat – no one seems worried
and the detail is very beautiful.
I'm writing this with experimental music playing
and suddenly I see how all art is aggression –
behind the brotherhood of man
creatures with shears spit and wait.

James Joyce Sings 'Il mio tesoro'

Something to warm your back teeth
even if your shirt's making its presence felt,
some piece of calculated impertinence –

My theory about *Hamlet* can drop
until I get these divisions right,
I mean the way McCormack gets them :
che sol di stragi e morti
nunzio voglio tornar
The Peace of the Fathers be with you
and all the browning photographs of Europe

Among the clean mountains the mad
are trained like roses on a trellis
                                pruned for love

My books are easier to write than read
and by God that's the proper division of labour

Nobody but me has produced literature
as great as music
                                    (I make an exception
of the author of *Hamlet*)

Do I hear some ijjit asking about
Proust and Synge and Pound
                                and a lot of names
I think I saw on raisin packets?

A fine tenor voice
the peace of great art

I never knew when to stop

If I'd been christened Stanislaus
I'd have claimed the throne of Poland

AFTER MARTIAL

I. xliii

What a host you are, Mancinus;
there we were, all sixty of us,
last night, decently invited guests
and this was the order of dishes
you pampered us with:

NO late-gathered grapes
NO apples sweet as honeycomb
NO ponderous ripe pears lashed to the branch
NO pomegranates the colour of blowing roses
NO baskets of best Sassina cheese
NO Picenian jars of olives

Only a miserable boar so small
a dwarf could have throttled it
one-handed. And nothing to follow,
no dessert, no sweet, no pudding, nothing . . .

We were the spectres, this was the feast,
a boar fit for the arena, duly
masticated by us –

I don't want to see you struggle
in your turn for a share of the crackling –
no, imitate instead
that poor devil Charidemus
who was shredded in the ring –
rather than miser eats boar
let's have boar eats miser:
bon appétit, my host of nothings,
I can almost feel the tushes in your throat.

II. lii

Dasius, chucker-out
at the Turkish Baths,
is a shrewd assessor;
when he saw big-titted
Spatale coming, he decided
to charge her entry for three
persons. What did she do?
Paid with pride of course.

II. lxxxvi

Because I don't attempt those modern poems
like lost papyri or Black Mountain Lyrics
stuffed with Court House Records, *non sequiturs*,
and advice on fishing; and since my lines
don't pun with mild obscenities in
the *Sunday Times*; nor yet ape Ezra's men
in spavined epics of the Scythian Marsh,
The Florentine Banking Scene, or hip-baths
in Northumberland; nor am I well-fledged
in the East European Translation Market,
whose bloody fables tickle liberal tongues;
despite this I make my claim to be a poet.
I'm even serious – you don't ask a runner
to try the high-jump, and if my trade is words
I'd be a misfit in the People Show.
From Liverpool to San Francisco, poets
are tuning to the Underground, a pop-
ulous place where laurels pale. My pleasure
is to please myself and if the Muses listen
I may find an ear or two to echo in.

III. xii

At dinner yesterday the smell was heaven
As we sat down to dine at seven;
Fabullus, our host, splashed the place with perfume,
More like a boudoir than a dining room,
But when it came to time to carve
He just sniffed the air and let us starve.
Fabullus, I said, please mind my seat,
I'm off to buy a winding sheet –
To be anointed but unable to ingest
Is the fate of a corpse, not of a guest.

III. xxxv

Instant Fish
by Phidias!
Add water
and they swim.

IV. xviii

Near the Vipsanian columns where the aqueduct
drips down the side of its dark arch,
the stone is a green and pulsing velvet
and the air is powdered with sweat
from the invisible faucet: there winter
shaped a dagger of ice, waited till
a boy looked up at the quondam stalactites,
threw it like a gimlet through his throat
and as in a murder in a paperback the clever
weapon melted away in its own hole. Where
have blood and water flowed before from one wound?
The story is trivial and the instance holy –
what portion of power has violent fortune
ever surrendered, what degraded circumstance
will she refuse? Death is everywhere
if water, the life-giving element,
will descend to cutting throats.

IV. xliv

Hear the testament of death:
yesterday beneath Vesuvius' side
the grape ripened in green shade,
the dripping vats with their viny tide
squatted on hill turf: Bacchus
loved this land more than fertile Nysa:
here the satyrs ran, this was Venus' home,
sweeter to her than Lacaedemon
or the rocks of foam-framed Cyprus.
One city now in ashes the great name
of Hercules once blessed, one other
to the salty sea was manacled.
All is cold silver, all fused in death
murdered by the fire of Heaven. Even
the Gods repent this faculty,
that power of death which may not be recalled.

V. lviii

Tomorrow is the time to live; tomorrow
        the tide will turn, says Postumus,
the golden days begin. Where's that tomorrow,
        Postumus, when will it arrive?
When it comes, won't it come as today,
        or is it hidden and must we search for it?
Perhaps the Parthians and Armenians
        have it locked in a sacred Ark;
maybe it's already as old as Priam
        or Nestor, and we'll meet it
coming round the other way. Perhaps it can
        be bought; how much then will it cost?
Tomorrow you will live, is that your
        firm intention? To live today
is already too late: *living*, Postumus,
        is what the wise man did yesterday.

VI. xxxix

It's good to have a quiver-full of kids, Cinna,
even these days –
to hell with the population explosion,
your little woman's done a great job.
There's just one matter I'd mention,
none of them is yours!
Nor your neighbours', nor your friend's,
nor the Elks', nor the Buffaloes', nor the Rotarians',
nor even an overnight hippy's in the sleep-out!
You can tell this lot were mapped
on unmade morning beds or sliding mats.
Here's one with steel-wool hair;
a gift from Santra the Cook;
that other with the joke-shop lips
and nostrils like cut-up avocadoes
is the spitting image of Pannichus the Wrestler
(I'll bet he was never late for rehearsals);
If you've ever seen Dama, the Baker's Son,
the original idle apprentice, knobbly, cataracted,
with the expression of a frozen cod,
then you'll recognize your own third son;
Number Four's the worst –
his forehead slopes like a loading chute,
his face is as white as a maggot, he's from an unlikely
source – your bed-mate Lygdus – so you can
use him the way you do his father,
it's a hallowed practice!
Consider the one with the coconut head
and ears like Eeyore, he's a perfect Identikit

of Cyrta the Cretin: two daughters, one dark,
one red-headed, you owe to Crotus the musician,
(some Ball he fluted at!) and Carpus the Bailiff
(it took him quite a time to deliver his injunction!).
        If it weren't that
    your other two servants, Coresus, and Dindymus,
        are eunuchs,
you'd be the Niobe of the Age. That's good luck, anyway,
Cinna. The gods won't punish, they'll only pity you.

VIII. xxix

To I.H.

The short poem signals
much suffering suppressed –
like the German Fleet at Scapa Flow,
only the flying pennants show!

Such terseness shames all us
chapter-and-versifiers –
but what's the point, since Fabers took
enough to make another book?

IX. xxxiii

Outside the Baths you hear applause –
Flaccus, you know the likely cause.
Connoisseurs love fine workmanship,
Maron has let his towel slip.

IX. liv

If I had hillside olives to fatten fieldfares
or Sabine woods strung with gins
to cruelly carry hot bodies from the sky
or could conduct like lightning
small morsels down on a stick, to walk
grand garnerer of their flutterings,
crop on crop in my meadows of death:
then I would send you these in token
of love, that you might bite their flesh
as it were mine. Alas, my fields are asphalt
and listen only to the songs of starlings,
the fidgeting of finches. The green
of tapered hedges hides the shrill sparrow,
here the magpie suffers an air-change
to death's bird, while the banished kite
haunts open fields, the only free man
in a heritage of dependence. Instead,
I offer you the imagination of birds
whose hard eye drops on the brown earth
without pardon: come to the start
of the world, we will deal with things cruelly
as we have love and an inclination to.

XI. xcix

Yours is a classic dilemma, Lesbia;
whenever you get up from your chair
your clothes treat you most indecently.
Tugging and talking, with right hand and left
you try to free the yards of cloth swept
up your fundament. Tears and groans
are raised to Heaven as the imperilled
threads are pulled to safety from
those deadly straits: the huge Symplegades
of your buttocks grip all that pass.
What should you do to avoid such
terrible embarrassment? Ask Uncle Val –
don't get up girl, and don't sit down!

XI. civ

You're my wife and you must fit my ways
Or leave the house: I don't keep fastdays,
Nor do I care how Tatius, Curius, Numa
Acted – founding fathers and consumer
Research heroes don't make me repent –
Sex is sex whichever way it's bent!
I prefer it served up elegantly:
A bladder full of wine's no enemy
To what we want to do (if it lies longer
At the point it makes the pleasure stronger),
But keep to water as you always choose,
Not caring to make love on top of booze,
And see what happens – half-way through your stint
You feel the urge, you disengage and sprint
To the loo, sad-eyed water-spiller, and then
You're back berating the appetites of men.
Another thing, I set no limit to
Love's duration: if before I'm through
Daylight's screaming in the floral pane
I say it's night-time still, so once again!
What's night to you? No night is dark enough
To get a head of steam up, no rough stuff
Keeps away the dragomans of sleep
Nor touch upon your haunches gets love's bleep!
It's bad enough, god knows, that you're inclined
To go to bed at half-past-bloody-nine
In opaque winceyette and cummerbund –
I like a girl that's naked, with her sun

Blazing its circuit for my solar lips
Or playing lost in space to fingertips;
For kissing I make doves my paradigm,
Beak to beak to dribble out the time;
Your sort of kissing is a woolly smother
Offered at breakfast to your old grandmother
And nothing will persuade you, neither words
Nor noises like those Kama Sutra birds,
To use a hand upon my other altar
Or try that *reservatus* style from Malta.
Consider the tradition of the service:
Andromache rode Hector like a war horse
While posted at the bedroom door the Phrygian
Slaves were masturbating (that's religion
For you), and in legendary days,
When heroes lived on earth and not in plays,
On Ithaca the while the Master slept
Penelope's well-instructed fingers kept
Their own appointment. You say that your arsehole
Is not for use, though good Cornelia, soul
Of Rome and glory of our past, reversed
Herself to Gracchus, Julia reimbursed
Her Pompey at the northern postern, and
Brutus's Portia served him contraband,
While long before the gods had Ganymede
To mix their drinks, proud Juno had agreed
To play the pretty boy to Jupiter –
Then why can't I with you, if Him with Her?

The gods and heroes gave all sex its due
But only abstinence will do for you:
I tolerate Lucretia by daylight
But I want Lais in my bed at night.

XII. xviii

Friend to friend, though from so far away,
greetings and happiness dear Juvenal
(malice aforethought, because we need
sharp natural spurs to our communication,
this prognostication), you're likely
at this moment to be tramping round
that speculator's mile, the loud Subura,
where Empire ticks are sucking blood (called rental)
from families and young provincials slink
home at evening clutching half a kipper;
or perhaps feeling the gravel of Diana's
hill under your thin-soled sandals; or then
fording the thresholds of the newly great,
aware of the sweaty draughts convected by
your toga – the big and little Caelian,
the sixpenny rides to newly elevated
broiler kings brooding on Palatine
penthouses: think of me and how you laughed
when I set off for Spain. I'm all right,
I'm a big frog in Bilbilis: many Decembers
spent in Rome find me back among
these unsophisticated craftsmen
of the heights, kneaders of gold and iron,
great auricular nomens if unable
to do much with the subjunctive. I'm lazy
here, a toff, I raise a spade just
to let it fall (the Government stroke we say);
I make friends in Boterdus and Platea
(I give you two whole pentameters

to laugh at these our Celtiberian names).
When I go to sleep, it's not just pausing,
getting back my strength to tackle tough-guy
patrons and insurgent tradesmen, it's real
long, self indulgent dreaming: huge un-
conscionable sleeps which even ten
o'clock can't founder. It's my post-war credit
for everything that Rome did; when I hear
some simple corporal at our feeble barracks
playing the Last Post on a wooden bugle
I think of all those stupid pushers listening
to bucinas in the Forum, girls on heat
and clever dicks from Thessaly touching
them up, wiping thumbs on blazers.
They can have it. I don't even have
a toga. If Aunt Lucy turns up at the door
with a basket full of cucumbers and lettuce
come to be useful at a lying-in,
I snatch a yard of ticking from the chair,
wrap it round me and play Jugurtha
or Caractacus upright at a Triumph.
They can't tell the difference, so why bother,
it's the man that makes the toga. Here they spend
hours just helping you, they really care
if you can stand the smell of oakwood smoke,
the savour of mosquito repellents.
My bailiff's wife crowns the dying fire
with my breakfast pot; I see her do it
opening half an eye to let the violet

air in, streaming from the upland plain.
My huntsman follows her, such a youth
as would set a dozen pens free-wheeling
in your bugger's land – one of our sycophants
would have him even if it cost as much
as an actor's villa in oiliest Misenum.
This man would be charmed if I
ventured as far as half-way to his rump;
in a grove of holy pines near Rome meeting him
you'd spend every waiting minute tearing
at your nails, and if he didn't come you'd
make from this fermata half a dozen
sub-Horatian odes. Here he's mine and so
I choose to close him only with my eyes.
He feeds my slaves, gathers up my acorns,
carries from snow-swollen Salo
all my washing water and then asks me
whether he should crop his hair. Here Juvenal
we see the seasons swing as never saw
Romans where the Tiber carries bodies:
this is how I live, friend, this is how
I love to live and am prepared to die.

XII. xxxi

This phalanx of pines, these demi-fountains,
this subtle pleaching, this irrigation system
ductile as a vein (water meadows under mountains),
and my twice-blooming roses richer than Paestum's,
the rare herb-garden – even in January, green –
my tame eel that snakes about its pond,
white dovecote outshone by its birds – I've been
a long time coming home and you, my fond
benefactress, dear Marcella, gave all this
to me. A miniature kingdom to do
with as I please. If Nausicaa with a kiss
should offer me her Father's gardens, you
need not worry: to everything that's grown
I give one answer, *I prefer my own.*

XIV. xxxix

A Bedside Light

I show but do not countenance what you do.
Douse me. The only record is in you.

LIVING IN A CALM COUNTRY

Living in a Calm Country

Each picture is a comic strip condensed.
You stare at Santa Fina on her bench
And the palisades are packed –
Looking is locking up, eyes are a fence.

A change of element to wallow in!
The swimmer wades through words – to him
Come doves and office pigeons,
Tu quoqueing his music, pinking his skin.

The difference is (again) the fact of time,
Such a lovely word that rhymes with rhyme:
Pictures stand still and still
Music composes the world, poems set lines.

Living in a calm country, which is me
Is not like architecture or the sea
Or diligence of diction or
Any Mixolydian matter, it's green, grey, green.

Then back to Santa Fina who gave up
Her life by giving up her seat, the luck
Of those the gods love, unlike
Myself at the window now, calm as a cup.

Playing with selfishness, I propose
Rules for the game, the most outrageous clothes
On truth, a cunning heart
Pumping in praise of time, as the world goes.

An Australian Garden

for Sally Lehmann

Here we enact the opening of the world
And everything that lives shall have a name
To show its heart; there shall be Migrants,
Old Believers, Sure Retainers; the cold rose
Exclaim perfection to the gangling weeds,
The path lead nowhere – this is like entering
One's self, to find the map of death
Laid out untidily, a satyr's grin
Signalling 'You are here': tomorrow
They are replanting the old court,
Puss may be banished from the sun-warmed stone.

See how our once-lived lives stay on to haunt us,
The flayed beautiful limbs of childhood
In the bole and branches of a great angophora –
Here we can climb and sit on memory
And hear the words which death was making ready
From the start. Such talking as the trees attempt
Is a lesson in perfectability. It stuns
The currawongs along the breaks of blue –
Their lookout cries have guarded Paradise
Since the expulsion of the heart, when man,
Bereft of joy, turned his red hand to gardens.

Spoiled Refugees nestle near Great Natives;
A chorus of winds stirs the pagoda'd stamens:
In this hierarchy of miniatures
Someone is always leaving for the mountains,

Civil servant ants are sure the universe
Stops at the hard hibiscus; the sun is drying
A beleaguered snail and the hydra-headed
Sunflowers wave like lights. If God were to plant
Out all His hopes, He'd have to make two more
Unknown Lovers, ready to find themselves
In innocence, under the weight of His green ban.

In the afternoon we change – an afterthought,
Those deeper greens which join the stalking shadows –
The lighter wattles look like men of taste
With a few well-tied leaves to brummel-up
Their poise. Berries dance in a southerly wind
And the garden tide has turned. Dark on dark.
Janus leaves are opening to the moon
Which makes its own grave roses. Old Man
Camellias root down to keep the sun intact,
The act is canopied with stars. A green sea
Rages through the landscape all the night.

We will not die at once. Nondescript pinks
Survive the death of light and over-refined
Japanese petals bear the weight of dawn's first
Insect. An eye makes damask on the dew.
Time for strangers to accustom themselves
To habitat. What should it be but love?
The transformations have been all to help
Unmagical creatures find their proper skins,

The virgin and the leonine. The past's a warning
That the force of joy is quite unswervable –
'Out of this wood do not desire to go'.

In the sun, which is the garden's moon, the barefoot
Girl espies her monster, all his lovely specialty
Like hairs about his heart. The dream is always
Midday and the two inheritors are made
Proprietors. They have multiplied the sky.
Where is the water, where the terraces, the Tritons
And the cataracts of moss? This is Australia
And the villas are laid out inside their eyes:
It would be easy to unimagine everything,
Only the pressure made by love and death
Holds up the bodies which this Eden grows.

On First Looking into Chapman's Hesiod

For 5p at a village fête I bought
Old Homer-Lucan who popped Keats's eyes,
Print smaller than the Book of Common Prayer
But Swinburne in the front, whose judgement is
Always immaculate. I'll never read a tenth
Of it in what life I have left to me
But I did look at *The Georgics*, as he calls
The Works and Days, and there I saw, not quite
The view from Darien but something strange
And balking – Australia, my own country
And its edgy managers – in the picture of
Euboeaen husbandry, terse family feuds
And the minds of gods tangential to the earth.

Like a Taree smallholder splitting logs
And philosophizing on his dangling billies,
The poet mixes hard agrarian instances
With sour sucks to his brother. Chapman, too,
That perpetual motion poetry machine,
Grinds up the classics like bone meal from
The abbatoirs. And the same blunt patriotism,
A long-winded, emphatic, kelpie yapping
About our land, our time, our fate, our strange
And singular way of moons and showers, lakes
Filling oddly – yes, Australians are Boeotians,
Thick as headlands, and, to be fair, with days
As robust as the Scythian wind on stone.

To teach your grandmother to suck eggs
Is a textbook possibility in New South Wales
Or outside Ascra. And such a genealogy too!
The Age of Iron is here, but oh the memories
Of Gold – pioneers preaching to the stringybarks,
Boring the land to death with verses and with
Mental Homes. 'Care-flying ease' and 'Gift-
devouring Kings' become the Sonata of the Shotgun
And Europe's Entropy; for 'the axle-tree, the quern,
The hard, fate-fostered man' you choose among
The hand castrator, kerosene in honey tins
And mystic cattlemen. The Land of City States
Greets Australia in a farmer's gods.

Hesiod's father, caught in a miserable village,
Not helped by magic names like Helicon,
Sailed to improve his fortunes, and so did
All our fathers. In turn, their descendants
Lacked initiative, other than the doctors' daughters
Who tripped to England. Rough-nosed Hesiod
Was sure of his property to a slip-rail –
Had there been grants, he'd have farmed all
Summer and spent winter in Corinth
At the Creative Writing Class. Chapman, too,
Would vie with Steiner for the Pentecostal
Silver Tongue. Some of us feel at home nowhere,
Others in one generation fuse with the land.

I salute him, then, the blunt old Greek whose way
Of life was as cunning as organic. His poet
Followers still make me feel deraciné
Within myself. One day they're on the campus,
The next in wide hats at a branding or
Sheep drenching, not actually performing
But looking the part and getting instances
For odes that bruise the blood. And history,
So interior a science it almost seems
Like true religion – who would have thought
Australia was the point of all that craft
Of politics in Europe? The apogee, it seems,
Is where your audience and its aspirations are.

'The colt, and mule, and horn-retorted steer' –
A good iambic line to paraphrase.
Long storms have blanched the million bones
Of the Aegean, and as many hurricanes
Will abrade the headstones of my native land:
Sparrows acclimatize but I still seek
The permanently upright city where
Speech is nature and plants conceive in pots,
Where one escapes from what one is and who
One was, where home is just a postmark
And country wisdom clings to calendars,
The opposite of a sunburned truth-teller's
World, haunted by precepts and the Pleiades.

Frogs at Lago di Bolsena

Having come down and run the car into sand
Not a foot from the reeds, the tense changes to
The Italian present and stories of Montefiascone
Are right for the first perambulation –
Only a few plastic bags floating and the smell
Of burning in the hills mild as eleven o'clock:
Then the frogs start – out there in the shallows, one
After another clamouring against official Nature.

For Nature is official here, its privilege extended
To recalcitrant weeds and momentous blossoms –
The Miracle of Bolsena struck from an open sky
And like a sunset the Host ran blood: what then
Can prevail upon the gentle waters, calm and bloodless,
When Christ's sanguinity fills the slaughterhouses
And the bone-dry churches? A corpse in damask
Holds the unsyntactical silence of despair.

Invisible and croaking in their plainness, the frogs
Speak of a similarly certain pain never
Lessening, and of the will to bring new pain
After, which this Italy has squared into art,
And which pilgrims with books in their hands try
To exorcize by long looks at lakes, judging
The far bank and marvellous islands until
The picture is captured and killed for their dreams.

The Descent into Avernus

Coming down from the serious hills upon
The Campanian flatlands, then we saw
The black lake where the stars reflected shone
Among the stagnant argosies of weed,
Small sulphur roses knocking at the shore
And swollen pumice jammed among the reeds.

This was the Leader's promise, a lake without
Birds or any living creature, fanned
By volcanic breath, the home of doubt;
Here we would camp and wait until a sign
Gave presence to the statutory land,
Blood from the earth or voices in a vine.

One of our purposes was to trace the smell,
That all-pervading smell of misery.
Some said it was the heroes dead in Hell
Smothered forever in their victims' flesh,
Others the pus of gods, rot in the Tree
Of Life no mortal creature could refresh.

That it was human where nothing human lived
Was everyone's hypothesis. The shades of armies
Stood behind the midday dazzle, sieved
From a glut of contours by the sun;
Beyond the line of salt some spindly trees
Waved like souls whose torments had begun.

The Leader made survival rules for all –
To be observers of the scene was our
Responsibility. In the long haul
To darkness, man would need supplies,
Rations which the dead could not devour,
Signals beyond his rational faculties.

And so upon the poisoned earth we sat,
The air itself a teeming oracle:
Man's soul might leave him like a cat,
His body come to carbon, yet somewhere
Behind this valley or that clambering hill
He'd find his true and disciplined despair.

Dreamtime

To the short-of-breath an apotheosis,
To come upstairs behind some Metternich
Of the party-giving world and still be
Recognized; your hostess, her rings shining,
Ready to rescue you out of corners.

This might be the door opening on a dream
Of a prosperous terrain where at last
Scenery germane to the heart is displayed:
Silos with clocks, the Norman church deaf
To the procession with the lilied corpse,

Half-Cockaigne among the seaweed grasses
And the animal moon awake all day,
Severe streets opening suddenly after fields
Of grain, the calm citizens ambling through
Huzzahs of troops for a near-sighted heir;

The parturition of the Princess golden
With balconies, and the revolutionaries' smithy
Watched by a bored spy; melancholy hours
In the cafés without even a betrayal
Or a sexual touch of foot or finger.

That is the scene, but it may change.
We may hurry to some Horatian outhouse
For the evening reading and discourse blood
On the pink-faced terrace, someone nearby
Playing the flute at a lizard listening.

Hate in the hills where the rebels practise
Games with black gourds, boredom in the library
At any time of day, but fear always,
Fear in everything. Responsibility for this
Is the question on each person's tongue.

They will try to get you to dream a new world
For them, one made clean by courage. You
May need to give a hostage as you do now
When you see approaching the perennial bore
Who is host to nature and a lord of change.

Cat's Fugue

What a clever moggie to tread only
        in the keys of G Minor and D Minor,
but then the gifted walk with care and flair
        as if on hot bricks; their bloodless
sleepwalking looks like exodus
        and the daggers are such dashing
footnotes. I chatted up a puss about Scarlatti
        but he had his Mason's secrets
and all I got was whiskers. Worthy men
        were walking by the gothic tulips,
sparrows purloined ears, so obviously
        the world was wired for sound.
Before you make your poem seem too twee
        I'll warn you, said the cat,
it's knowing when to stretto, how to keep
        your counter-subjects simple,
What to do when grandeur blows your mind –
        also, you'll notice that my fur
lies one way, so please don't brush it backwards
        and call the act experiment.
That sour cat was dead against our century
        and I was so ambitious,
I bought a cosmological notebook,
        Zinoviev's new machine
and a glossary of the German terms in Joyce –
        I'm in retirement till I make
my violent masterpiece; it's about a cat
        bigger than Bulgakov's, east

of Jeoffry in the night sky of the Lord;
        it stalks like plague along the grass
fathering history on the post-diluvial age –
        named Jesus at the whole Jerusalem,
the Day of Modernism dawns; professors touched
        by wings fly purring to the moon.
These are its juvenilia and in Horatian
        retrospect I see the cat
restored to its domestic stalking one salt
        Iberian morning in the light
when genius saddened at the cold keyboard
        is jacked with white and black –
again our dainty-footed man's companion
        strikes a balance with the dust
and props the world against its weary gravity.

Ode to Afternoon

A command to the middle-aged,
you shall write disguised love poems
so that the young may respect you
when the truth is known

They will ensex your abstracts
wink knowingly at all
the stale erudition
which so enrages your critics

You must make capital out of despair:
real pain is never art,
turn instead to quotidian tasks,
Grub Street at the obsessional!

In your review of *The Romance of Linear B*,
notice that all the texts are Official Art,
the numbers of the king's combs and cattle –
their songs you must imagine for yourself

Of *The Eighteen Chorales*, there is much love of God –
you alone have cracked the cypher
and know what he meant when he told the soul
to bedeck itself for its bridegroom

In the middle of *The Children's Crusade*
you may put two adolescents under a tree
poking bits of bark down each other's front,
music by Puccini, the sun declining

Having set the scene, you are in the Land
of Afternoon. Sex, if it comes, will be late,
up some stairs following a nervous lunch,
her eyes like a Florentine postcard

In the afternoon they came unto a land
in which it seemed always afternoon:
The fathers were at the races
and the lawnmowers ran all over the hills

Afternoon men in the morning of the world,
we donate our three score and ten
to a beleaguered maturity –
province of afghan hounds and honeydew

Mother, the girls you warned me of
are waiting behind the rector's hedge,
I can hear their voices: they are content
with the usual menagerie

Home of averages where human kind
cannot bear very much reality
but the sun is always over the yard-arm
and we are for the dark

Der Untergang des Abendlandes
is still a best seller though it sounds
better with a stierhorn's blast
than a song at twilight

These quotations will keep nobody warm,
so put away the deck chairs
and the half-finished poem
and return to your research

Which was into the lineaments
of great fiction, and began
with the motherless boy
circuiting his grown-up garden:

Huge tears are in the pond,
every hurt has a face like a flower –
that will be music across the road
from the long-dead birthday party

O sprays of scent and my blue aunts,
I am coming with my excuses ready:
I was reading down in the boatshed,
how shall we get through the afternoon?

That Depression is an Abstract

That depression is an Abstract
is my doctor's view, who watches me open
one ear on a hinge and looks with interest
at a countryside of flowers and barges
and squares of green each carrying a cow –
                        None of this is necessary
he says in his subtle lower case,
you have landlines to ten capitals.
                        Good thinking,
bring the calabashes of iced wine
and the little sausages, I reply.
                        Lie on this couch
and tell me what Europe said to you.
                        She showed me an olive hillside
with the minty dead trowelled in a wall
and scented black steadying itself
for picnics on Mt Erebus.
                        She took my brown eyes
for gristle, something she could never swallow,
they had held tears at one age –
                        She said, my son,
I would name a river for you
if only I had one left –
I loved your galloping through the evening fields,
your snout plating over and your gills
forming where the love-bites were.
                        I saw the old castle
where deformity took itself as subject
and wrote God into the moon. Aunty Dolour

was my university and our good dog
played the Wolf of Gubbio
at the back door.
                    Eventually, doctor,
we must come down to cases
but my memory is bad.
                    There are these polemics
you write against the new art –
'Why persecutest thou me?'
You have a cruel masterpiece
crying to get out, Saints Cosmas
and Damian healing a Rider
Haggard impi.
                    Six pounds fifty
an hour should clear your head.
Indeed, as the sun stretched along my side,
I gazed at the advertisements –
                    I do not feel depressed
although it is old in May and not
my time of year.
                    I would like you
to use plain syntax and straight words
and to practise your left-hand scales!
                    They fell from my eyes
in the first reels of eternity,
my bones were hollow before the lark's –
having paid and spoken and been listened to,
I have my certificate of going back,
guaranteeing it as it was then,

coming down a winding road of villas
to the Badia, the lodge gates plaqued
'Domenico Cimarosa lived here
in 1779', and then the black sky breaking,
seeing a face I loved and knowing
it had no respect for me, seeing my father
in the rain trying to clip the bougainvillea.
                    Until death
the abstracts will have silver faces,
baroque lanterns like the moon,
terror pressed into depression,
                    you and you and you,
father, son and lover of the world.

The Settembrini Waltz

Time was, the fund of knowledge
Led to the barricades
And not, as in this college,
To making higher grades.

That was the great Cenacle
When dew formed in the night
Would coruscate and sparkle
On police boots polished bright.

When pages out of Balzac
And things the Fathers wrote
Were more than some Old Pals Act
Or urban guerilla's quote.

But polish up your Fanon
And keep your Brechtwerk gay,
The latest sine qua non
Is Ethnic Shadowplay.

Hearing the Appassionata
Sapped Lenin's will to fight,
But Cage's cool self-starter
Sits squadrons down to write.

Let's end it one cold morning
With bullets in a bed,
All ironies self-scorning
And liberal Europe dead.

THE COST OF SERIOUSNESS

The Picture of Nobody

We are always being framed somewhere. A camera, an eye
Of memory is recounting inches along from the pea-trellis,
The cement-block fence, the rotary clothes-line: a leg
Is not quite where it seemed and an arm forward on the thigh
Strikes a posture more aggressive than the smiling face.

Then, beside the church where a clapped-out pigeon fell
To be picked up by a not-very-poor-looking Italian – was
She standing higher on the steps, or perhaps just out of sight
To the left? The Hotel de Beurs was surely closer to the canal,
The photograph should smell of cleansing and dark cloths.

Years after, another presence makes itself felt, someone
Who wasn't there when we bought the angle-poise lamp
And were snapped in the street, a shape which vanished
From the wharf-side beer garden and the Japanese bridge
Over an English river – now he seems so very like me.

A sentimental assumption. We put up our own coordinates,
The bars of our prison. Her own picture the doppelgänger,
She was already haunting those September stones with
Her death, just as at seven the teeth stick out which
Later slope in, rodent-like. The wave freezes at its crest.

Bring the coordinates together to get us out of unhappiness.
We are in limbo. And his picture is quite clear now.
He will move to the new album, the later, more hopeful
Photos over the same ground. Three cats on top of each other
Behind a grille in Venice, or a window of star-shaped ice-creams.

No wonder there are ghosts. What we leave behind is deadly.
The melody is played, a poisonous, long-lasting scent
Circles the garden. Spring again. Our friend has borrowed
A loved face to bring the bad news to the still living:
There is nobody else in the picture, yet fear looks out.

Waiting for Rain in Devon

Rain here on a tableau of cows
might seem a return to everyday –
why, you can almost poach
the trout with your hands,
their element has so thickened!
Something has emerged from dreams
to show us where we are going,
a journey to a desolate star.
Come back, perennial rain,
stand your soft sculptures in our gardens
for the barefoot frogs to leap.

The Easiest Room in Hell

At the top of the stairs is a room
one may speak of only in parables.

It is the childhood attic,
the place to go when love has worn away,
the origin of the smell of self.

We came here on a clandestine visit
and in the full fire of indifference.

We sorted out books and let the children
sleep here away from creatures.

From its windows, ruled by willows,
the flatlands of childhood stretched
to the watermeadows.

It was the site of a massacre,
of the running down of the body
to less even than the soul,
the tribe's revenge on everything.

It was the heart of England
where the ballerinas were on points
and locums laughed through every evening.

Once it held all the games,
Inconsequences, Misalliance, Frustration,
even *Mendacity*, *Adultery* and *Manic Depression*.

But that was just its alibi,
all along it was home,
a home away from home.

Having such a sanctuary
we who parted here
will be reunited here.

You asked in an uncharacteristic note,
'Dwell I but in the suburbs
of your good pleasure?'

I replied, 'To us has been allowed
the easiest room in hell.'

Once it belonged to you,
now it is only mine.

An Angel in Blythburgh Church

Shot down from its enskied formation,
This stern-faced plummet rests against the wall;
Cromwell's soldiers peppered it and now the death-
watch beetle has it in thrall.

If you make fortunes from wool, along
The weeping winter foreshores of the tide,
You build big churches with clerestories
And place angels high inside.

Their painted faces guard and guide. Now or
Tomorrow or whenever is the promise –
The resurrection comes: fix your eyes halfway
Between Heaven and Diss.

The face is crudely carved, simplified by wind;
It looks straight at God and waits for orders,
Buffeted by the organ militant, and blasted
By choristers and recorders.

Faith would have our eyes as wooden and as certain.
It might be worth it, to start the New Year's hymn
Allowing for death as a mere calculation,
A depreciation, entered in.

Or so I fancy looking at the roof beams
Where the dangerous beetle sails. What is it
Turns an atheist's mind to prayer in almost
Any church on a country visit?

Greed for love or certainty or forgiveness?
High security rising with the sea birds?
A theology of self looking for precedents?
        A chance to speak old words?

Rather, I think of a woman lying on her bed
Staring for hours up to the ceiling where
Nothing is projected – death the only angel
        To shield her from despair.

An Exequy

In wet May, in the months of change,
In a country you wouldn't visit, strange
Dreams pursue me in my sleep,
Black creatures of the upper deep –
Though you are five months dead, I see
You in guilt's iconography,
Dear Wife, lost beast, beleaguered child,
The stranded monster with the mild
Appearance, whom small waves tease,
(Andromeda upon her knees
In orthodox deliverance)
And you alone of pure substance,
The unformed form of life, the earth
Which Piero's brushes brought to birth
For all to greet as myth, a thing
Out of the box of imagining.
This introduction serves to sing
Your mortal death as Bishop King
Once hymned in tetrametric rhyme
His young wife, lost before her time;
Though he lived on for many years
His poem each day fed new tears
To that unreaching spot, her grave,
His lines a baroque architrave
The Sunday poor with bottled flowers
Would by-pass in their mourning hours,
Esteeming ragged natural life
('Most dearly loved, most gentle wife'),
Yet, looking back when at the gate

And seeing grief in formal state
Upon a sculpted angel group,
Were glad that men of god could stoop
To give the dead a public stance
And freeze them in their mortal dance.

The words and faces proper to
My misery are private – you
Would never share your heart with those
Whose only talent's to suppose,
Nor from your final childish bed
Raise a remote confessing head –
The channels of our lives are blocked,
The hand is stopped upon the clock,
No one can say why hearts will break
And marriages are all opaque:
A map of loss, some posted cards,
The living house reduced to shards,
The abstract hell of memory,
The pointlessness of poetry –
These are the instances which tell
Of something which I know full well,
I owe a death to you – one day
The time will come for me to pay
When your slim shape from photographs
Stands at my door and gently asks
If I have any work to do
Or will I come to bed with you.
O scala enigmatica,

I'll climb up to that attic where
The curtain of your life was drawn
Some time between despair and dawn –
I'll never know with what halt steps
You mounted to this plain eclipse
But each stair now will station me
A black responsibility
And point me to that shut-down room,
'This be your due appointed tomb.'

I think of us in Italy:
Gin-and-chianti-fuelled, we
Move in a trance through Paradise,
Feeding at last our starving eyes,
Two people of the English blindness
Doing each masterpiece the kindness
Of discovering it – from Baldovinetti
To Venice's most obscure jetty.
A true unfortunate traveller, I
Depend upon your nurse's eye
To pick the altars where no Grinner
Puts us off our tourists' dinner
And in hotels to bandy words
With Genevan girls and talking birds,
To wear your feet out following me
To night's end and true amity,
And call my rational fear of flying
A paradigm of Holy Dying –
And, oh my love, I wish you were

Once more with me, at night somewhere
In narrow streets applauding wines,
The moon above the Apennines
As large as logic and the stars,
Most middle-aged of avatars,
As bright as when they shone for truth
Upon untried and avid youth.

The rooms and days we wandered through
Shrink in my mind to one – there you
Lie quite absorbed by peace – the calm
Which life could not provide is balm
In death. Unseen by me, you look
Past bed and stairs and half-read book
Eternally upon your home,
The end of pain, the left alone.
I have no friend, or intercessor,
No psychopomp or true confessor
But only you who know my heart
In every cramped and devious part –
Then take my hand and lead me out,
The sky is overcast by doubt,
The time has come, I listen for
Your words of comfort at the door,
O guide me through the shoals of fear –
'Fürchte dich nicht, ich bin bei dir.'

The Delegate

In the garden (it was always a garden)
there is the punishment of remembrance.
I pray you love, remember. And quote me
the many things which might come to you
on your own death bed.
                                        I was there
even in our worst hour – the wreaths
and the mis-named name competing with
the other mourners' flowers upon
the crematorium slabs. I am divided
into an infinity of myself, pieces
for everywhere – especially that damp day,
that insistence on seriousness.
We shall never be so serious again.
But this frees you for levity today,
and perhaps a little licensed selfishness.
Take this gift of despair – what can
a ghost give but remembrance and
forgetfulness in the right proportions?

Never to puff up those sloping headlands
watching the children ahead negotiating
the lanes of the wide bay: never
the afternoon sun straining
the bedroom light to a tint distinctly
like gin: never more the in-flight panic,
refusing to see omens in our food
or the number of letters in the month.
are just parts of my docility

as I go back. I am always receding,
my ambition is to accomplish
non-existence, to go out and close the door
on ever having been.
I am doing it in death
as I did in life – but it's so hard.
I cannot forget unless you remember,
pin down each day and weighted eye
with exact remorse. After fifteen years'
convergence, now we may draw apart
and face our different exits.

So I am your delegate
at the screaming hours: I walk alone
among the plains of hell. We dream here
in the skin of our deeds: such changes
as the schoolgirl saw in her body
are metamorphoses of the gods.
First I went back,
a quick change in the early morning
with my blood running into frost.
Now the reduction is set at smaller things –
I may even become the healthy strider
or flamenco dancer, but I must reduce, reduce,
become so small that I escape the eye
of god. There is no peace here, or on earth.
You will know
how the mind works at poems, feels ideas
as tissue – but, alas, the ceremony here

is different. I am not what you remember,
the snapshots in time and sunshine,
nor even the angry and accusing face
at breakfast, the suddenly delivered tone
of hope along a Venetian calle on a Sunday –
I am made fiction
by my needs: the brain changing in the garden
to a bush of thorns, a dream looking for
its dreamer, murder always at the end
of every vista. A letter now, headed
'Malcontenta, Orto Chiuso', a puff-adder's face
as I prop myself against the dying mirror
viewing disgust with satisfaction.
Breaking an egg-cup,
learning to give up, crying at the sight
of a withered seahorse pinned to the wall:
all those afternoons of hope and all those gardens,
no wonder I cannot escape now.
After a year in office,
your delegate has found this court
a place of ashes and the matches
played by moonlight cruel games.
But I have an immense truth to give you –
In the end, we are condemned
only for our lack of talent.
There is no morality,
no metered selfishness, or cowardly fear.
What we do on earth is its own parade
and cannot be redeemed in death. The pity

of it, that we are misled. By mother,
saying her sadness is the law, by love,
hiding itself in evenings of ethics,
by despair, turning the use of limbs
to lockjaw.

The artist knows this.
He is being used despite himself. The truth
is a story forcing me to tell it. It is not
my story or my truth. My misery
is on a colour chart – even my death
is a chord among the garden sounds.

And in this garden, love,
there will be forgiveness, when
we can forgive ourselves. 'Remember me,
but ah forget my fate.' Tell me like music
to the listeners. 'I would not know her in that dress.'
The days I lived through change to words
which anyone may use. When you arrive
I shall have done your work for you.

Forgetting will not be hard,
but you must remember still. Evenings
and mad birds cross your face,

everything must be re-made.

The Cost of Seriousness

Once more I come to the white page of art
to discover what I know
and what I presume I feel
about those forgettable objects words.
We begin with penalties:
the cost of seriousness will be death.

Not just naming death again to stoke fires,
but thinking of suicide
because life or art won't work
and words trying to help, Mallarmé-like,
undefine themselves and say
things out of the New Physics: self-destruct!

Which is why the artist must play, but if
he does he mustn't rule-change
and say, 'Unless you agree
to Pound's huge seriousness I shan't go
on living, and meanwhile we
are an élite of experimenters,

to whom someones in the city must pay
homage, dons give neat memos
and our correspondents pile
up hagiography in magazines –'
A public worthy of its
artists would consist of whores and monsters

So, to turn impatience into anger
          and want to punish slow minds
          or walk through our museums
with a clock ends up as despair or a
          professorship in exile,
the world as solipsistic as ever.

At which you may ask (ungentle reader)
          why does he avoid the point?
          After great vindication
coming through B-Flat this way will never
          be the same, and so the earth
changes while we stand by a grave and mourn.

Yes, but the earth stays the same too, greeting
          leaves and their sons each season
          just seasonally; the boat
for Venice idles at the green-furred wharf
          carrying the body of
the composer Grimace (Ettore),

as timetable-conscious as if it had
          on board a scientist who
          could make a food crop of grass,
and I have come no closer to my goal
          of doing without words, that
pain may be notated some real way.

Seriousness – ah, *quanta pena mi*
costi! I note from a card
that hills are dyed purple by
a weed named Paterson's Curse. That is in
New South Wales. The dead may pass
their serious burdens to the living.

Gertrude Stein at Snails Bay

(from 'Three Transportations')

I am Miss Stein
and this bay is mine

I am Miss Stein (pronounced Steen)
and this sea is green

Americans do not like
European pronunciation

I live in Europe because Americans
do not like Europeans

I do not live in America
because Europeans do not like Americans

I am in Australia because
I hear you have an opera
and I am searching for snails

I am not here to buy your paintings

I am in Snails Bay to find snails

Although there are no snails in Snails Bay
there are buses behind me
and children in front of me
and sea in front of the children

They tell me this is Arbor Day

No, I do not drop my aitches

Nothing can be done in the face
of ordinary unhappiness

Above all, there is nothing to do in words

I have written a dozen books
to prove nothing can be done in words

A great artist may fall off an inner alp
but I will not roll down this gentle bank

I would not give a cook book for his alp

I have a message for the snails
of New South Wales

You will never know
which of you is Shakespeare

Yes, I am a disagreeable old woman
who talks selfishly and strangely
and writes down words in a peculiar order

It is to prevent unhappiness escaping
and poisoning the world

How do you define
the truth, Miss Stein?

A snail has not the right to say
it will or won't: it must obey

With the buses and the children and the sea
I have nothing to do

I am an observer,
I observe the blue and you

I see an immense rain
washing pebbles up the beach
and evacuating misery

The plane for America is a sort of star

The Painters' Banquet

They came with their gifts of the senses
And of the groves planted for them by God
In the retina; they knelt by sandy waters
And saw a violin shore, a fronded region
Of high responding light, rosella afternoon;
They gossiped in laps, lay under umbrellas
Of the tumid shade; they told colours
In every story. When the pelican glided,
They overcame light, where the daisy unpeeled
They saw graveclothes. There were many
With eyelashes like Veronese's fans,
Others sat solitary as meat on a plate
Waiting for heaven to happen. Change,
Said some, was the way of their world,
Animals answering the call of light
Under Hyperion's crag. But, said several,
It is the unchanging we celebrate,
Sirocco afternoons, gods hard-pressed
By their abstract eyes. Dangerous modes
In all weather when obsessionals walk
To a favourite spur above the land –
Below them kingdoms boil and they find
Twisting paths through middle space.
This is the sumptuous gallery of those
Who have eaten the world. Oh the ochre,
Burnt sienna, the pulverising red
Which rocks have earned from the sun –
In little spaghetti-making towns,

The dead artificers' creations burn
All sophistry from pilgrim's eyes.

It was a wonderful party to be at.
We write our thank-you letters
In the world's far-reaching galleries.
Who will clean up now? All the water
In the reservoirs won't remove the stain
From Golgotha. We think back instead:
Little Andrea has drawn a sheep
With a bright stone upon a smooth-faced rock.
Lucky for him a Medici is passing.
Soon the banquet will be set again.

Non Piangere, Liù

A card comes to tell you
you should report
to have your eyes tested.

But your eyes melted in the fire
and the only tears, which soon dried,
fell in the chapel.

Other things still come –
invoices, subscription renewals,
shiny plastic cards promising credit –
not much for a life spent
in the service of reality.

You need answer none of them.
Nor my asking you for one drop
of succour in my own hell.

Do not cry, I tell myself,
the whole thing is a comedy
and comedies end happily.

The fire will come out of the sun
and I shall look in the heart of it.

The Lying Art

It is all rhetoric rich as wedding cake
and promising the same bleak tears
when what was asked for but not recognized
shows its true face after a thousand breakfasts.

This, not Miss Moore's disclaimer, tells me
why I too dislike it. It is paid to distract us,
to tell the man disappointed by his mother
that he too can be a huge cry-baby.

Think of its habit of talking to gods
but saying only pastoral things. Real pain
it aims for, but can only make gestures,
the waste of selling-short, the 'glittering'.

I want you to be happy, you say,
but poetry brings in childhood on its horse,
the waves of parrots and the Delphic eyes,
and is never there when the scab is picked.

Music gets the better of it, since music is all lies.
Lies which fill the octave. Chromatic space
in verse turns out to be the ego's refractions,
truth always stained by observation.

So this argument goes in cut-up prose,
four lines to each part. I will not say
metric or stanzas or anything autonomous,
but keep to discontent, a nearly truthful art.

And what has this to do with poetry? Inroads
into rhetoric. The ugly and the disappointed
painting their faces with words; water showing
God's love to the beautiful – no way of changing.

Then we might as well make the best of
dishonesty, accept that all epithalamiums
are sugar and selfishness. Our world
of afterwards will have no need of lies.

A Lecture by my Books

You cannot write tonight. We own all
the words you will ever need to make a shape
of permanence. But they were used by
men who felt along the lines
to life. We are dead
who kept the watch for you while your landscapes burned,
we stand like stelae
on the road to hell. Fear us.

And market us in dreams. We
are the finished phrase, the play of gesture stopped
before one death. See this gasping soul
declare a total library of meaning
less than a nerve end,
Anacreon's grave a house
of roots and the reaching out goodbye
your only poem.

From *Julius Caesar* and the laws
of aspic hardening, the heart will
snatch a vocabulary –
'I just want to be dead' – and all the novels
fry tonight. What did
poor Carrington find in her shotgun barrels?
Words for ending words,
the picture of nobody there.

In this garden of categories
a night rose withers –
it was the spume of Rilke,
words lying on the carpet where a planet
winters and the dapper genius
welcomes god to his
own twentieth century: a rich tapis
for tongue-tied democracy.

To be the actuaries of hope,
not so many graveyards of trees but gestures
in a terrible silence –
To be recognized,
a man, a woman
and a relationship. But the cat
has seen through their plan. He knows they have only
printed their hearts. He reads knees.

Here are the lines of a last conspiracy.
Listen to our words,
there are no others. Can you write now?
The brain's a neologism of rare aspect
but it isn't quite music.
We've sat on your walls and heard
the moon cry for the dead, poor centaurs,
poor Humpty Dumpties.

Roman Incident

The two of us, tired after a night
of quarrelling and making love
to make up quarrels and not quite
succeeding, first found the airline
in a Roman street and made our bookings,
then moved in a slightly drunken way
through the boring Via Veneto
to the Borghese Gardens. So far, so much.
An ice-cream eaten, a path adopted –
she must simply lie down and sleep
in the grass and I who couldn't sleep
stay there beside her. A woman sleeping
makes me lonely: I saw love in her face
and I had seen love die before,
so I left her and walked across other lovers
to the Gallery. All that awful
Caravaggiesque paint and Cardinal Scipio
straight from the movies. At last,
a marvellous Carpaccio of a whore,
a quick look at my watch, thinking of
her lying there in the grass,
resolved to make one circuit and then leave –
but here I came upon a picture,
Dosso Dossi's *Melissa*, apotheosis
of the watching female and her autumn shades.
Left hand lower corner a labrador
ready to nuzzle to his master
in stockbroker Surrey and in the woods,
russet with the ferns of terra firma,

the enclosed bodies of men reassuming
their uncanted shapes. Garrulous
as a Fabian hostess, the lady ties
your looking with her colours –
the painter has borrowed Titian's later dyes
for pure frivolity. Armorial death
enchants when this Melissa looks:
frozen jibes from long-running
civil epics out of Italy, Ariosto's suspense,
Tasso's cracks on the head – Dossi warms them
in his hand. Life is a spell
and when we wake from it
the animals of our senses stand
with us in play-power paradise.
Visit Melissa's extra-mural zoo,
you'll find yourself hiding in shrubbery
when a truthful woman summons you.
Standing frozen before her on a plinth
of grief and awkwardness, I tried to cry,
to force water from my eyes, so that
Melissa might turn me back to manhood –
that, I said, is what I want. Magic, fortune, love:
the luck to be kissed and smiled on
no matter what ridiculous wizard
corks up my heart. To mother,
wife and all the sultry dead I prayed,
lead me to the enchantress whose one kiss
undoes the tactless misery of self.
When I got back

to our flattened patch of grass, she'd gone
and I was desperate. Of a sudden
I heard her call my name and saw her body
approaching on the path. Her sleep had eased her
so we walked to lunch and an afternoon's
sightseeing via Pantheon and Forum,
ahead of us the night and our hotel.

ENGLISH SUBTITLES

My Old Cat Dances

He has conceived of a Republic of Mice
and a door through the fire,
parables of the reinstatement
of his balls. But not this night.
Isn't there a storm in the light bulb,
condors circling the kittens' meals
on the television screen?
He heard once that people wearied of
each other to escape unhappiness.
In his lovely sufficiency
he will string up endless garlands
for the moon's deaf guardians.
Moving one paw out and yawning,
he closes his eyes. Everywhere
people are in despair. And he is dancing.

Returning

Nobody feels well after his fortieth birthday
But the convalescence is touched by glory
So that history's truculent deeds of hate
Are lived through in dreams, the story
Followed to the investigator's hut, pain seen
Through a window on its knees, late
Help lost over marram dunes or never
Felt at the deliverance on a screen.

Marvellous means of escaping time and time's
Chosen people: sleep on the knowledge of
God's monsters! The school of love and crimes
Is open every night and the sedentary
Heir of men of action dashes off
A sonnet before execution. What you see
Is coiled in an uneventful past, rough
Justice of the body's failures, a commentary.

Yet never daring enough, even those hours
When the timid rule of truth relents
And every written word is without sense
As in some ultimate avant-gardish shape –
The apostle of plain dullness has powers
Of arrest and will use them; nightmares
Are prized categories too, a southern rape
Modelled in blood but with a classic tense.

It is time to recompose the face
Into a serious map, the children now
Envied creatures across a room, the case
Being settled for the present. Home is
The veteran of the adjectival run,
His images intact. He has learned how
To live another day and wakes, ringed
By the golden wallpaper of the sun.

Sonata Form: The Australian Magpie

It makes a preliminary statement
with its head to one side and an eye
far too large to be seemly.

It is no relation to the English magpie
yet is decently black and white,
upstaging its cousin the currawong.

Its opening theme is predation.
What it scavenges is old cake
soaked in dew, but might be eyes.

Such alighting and strutting
across the mown grass of the Ladies' College!
Siege machines are rolling near.

Bustle in a baking tin,
a feast of burnt porridge –
the children are growing on their way to school.

You can upbraid the magpie,
saying, 'What do you know of Kant?'
It might shift a claw an inch or two.

It can tell when an overlord is unhappy.
When one sweeps out in tears to clatter
the petrol mower, magpie flies off.

But never flies far. Big feet
are moving to their place in dreams –
a little delay in the sun won't count.

We have certainly heard this theme before,
the sound of homecoming. Anticipation
needs a roof, plus a verandah for magpies.

Are these the cries of love or of magpies
sighting food? Some things about desire
call for explicit modern novels.

Magpie talk: Nation, National, Nationalist!
In this tongue its name is legion.
We speak English ourselves, with a glossary.

The coda, alas. It can be Brucknerian.
We say the end is coming. The magpie
has found its picture in an encyclopaedia.

Where can there be nature enough
to do without art? In despair, the poet
flies to the top of a camphor laurel.

Girl and magpie leave him in the tree.
Tomorrow a trip down the coast for her
and spaghetti rings left out for the bird.

What I Have Written I Have Written

It is the little stone of unhappiness
which I keep with me. I had it as a child
and put it in a drawer. There came
a heap of paper to put beside it,
letters, poems, a brittle dust
of affection, sallowed by memory.

Aphorisms came. Not evil, but
the competition of two goods
brings you to the darkened room.
I gave the stone to a woman
and it glowed. I set my mind
to hydraulic work, lifting words
from their swamp. In the light from the stone
her face was bloated. When she died
the stone returned to me, a present
from reality. The two goods
were still contending. From wading pools
the children grew to darken
gardens with their shadows. Duty
is better than love, it suffers no betrayal.

Beginning again, I notice
I have less breath but the joining
is more golden. There is a long way to go,
among gardens and alarms,
after-dinner sleeps peopled by toads
and all the cries of childhood.
Someone comes to say my name

has been removed from the Honourable
Company of Scribes. Books in the room
turn their backs on me.

Old age will be the stone and me together.
I have become used to its weight
in my pocket and my brain.
To move it from lining to lining
like Beckett's tramp,
to modulate it to the major
or throw it at the public –
all is of no avail. But I'll add
to the songs of the stone. These words
I take from my religious instruction,
complete responsibility –
let them be entered in the record,
What I have written I have written.

The Future

It is always morning in the big room
but the inhabitants are very old.
Crooking her finger on a watering-can,
a precise figure of regret, no wisp
of her silver hair disturbed, drips succour
on a cat-predated plant. Words here
are shredded like its silver leaves,
they are epitomes of chanciness,
none will get you through the day.
When the sun fills the windows with its
misleading call to truth, the old woman
changes to a young girl, then to a man
from a novel looking up to ask
why things have gone so very wrong.
I am allowed, as if this were a dream,
to join them on their tableau.
We do not die, they say, but harden
into frescoes. This is what the future means,
her seeking me on her knees, poignant
as a phrase from a Victorian novel
or farewell spoken beyond a watercourse,
lyrical erotica I have no talent for –
Just the one room brightening, to which
hasten all the relatives of insecurity,
talking of my brief Bohemian days:
To be poised as the long-necked swan
or collared badger while the work
of worldliness is done, to stay the same

after the sun has gone, waiting merely
for light to show us up; the future
is to stand still with one gesture held,
a white glove entering a confluence.

Alcestis and the Poet

As the little blue-tongued lizard runs across
The floor and clambers on the cushions, so I
Have spent my life in your service. I have
Risen from beds of my own melancholy to grant
Your distress an audience, heard the chorus of self
Desert its lord to swell your tragedy. It wasn't
Self-effacement but a bonding-up of time. We
Start with bodies from our wounded parents, not knowing
That the early flesh is useless, that its greyness
Towards death is what we love in it. So,
As young Shakespearean gestures, we glow among our feelings
And are pointless. Then, as the shades of madness
Intervene, we become important. Voices singing German ask
'Watchman, what of the night?'; geniuses ever upward tell
Of willing death, of lining tombs for study, Chattertons
Who persist in books. The soft arrival counts. Now,
When the rake of afternoon has laid the shadows,
We are ready to do each other service. Can
I march tongue-tied to the end; will you
Find the inexplicable, the out-of-reach-of-art
Intensity you mourn for outside Hades? I took
Your place and watched the stories grow. But it
Was no more than giving up a good position
In the queue – we are all for darkness. Death
Is in the small print, as Stevie Smith showed,
Ringing the word in galleys on her final bed –
Thus the loving woman does her duty and is
Woven into legend. The king sits in his kitchen,
Not certain if the world knows of her sacrifice,

Though don't his cats despise him? Are you there
Where each new disappointment makes you think that life
Is geared to reparation? And this time who is
Hercules? The joy of giving up, of saying sweetly,
'It could never have worked – real love must be
Thrown away or it will burn us.' The rest
Is timing. On the moon, they say, we find
The things we've sacrificed, pristine and waxing. Such dreams
Are cheats. Sited in great art, but tearful still,
The creatures that we are make little gestures, then
Go to nothing. The wind urges the trees to sigh
For us: it is not a small thing to die,
But looking back I see only the disappointed man
Casting words upon the page. Was it for this
I stepped out upon the stairs of death obediently?

Addio Senza Rancor

'Such past and reticence!' – George Macbeth

Two girls in their last year at school,
in the back row since they are taller,
stay young in the autograph album
which has slipped into sight from among
the fallen contents of the bookcase. Here are
the ingredients of sorrow, forever renewing
itself by generations – one was to die
at forty-one and the other at forty-four.

Not young by the standards of the world's unfairness,
only by those of our spoiled corner of it.
Why do we go on manufacturing misery,
waking when it cries, cleaning it for school,
clapping at the prize giving? The new girls
are in their mothers' clothes and the new fathers
stripping for the shining theatre instruments –
Unhappiness lives on, depression dies early.

Friends and lovers, kept apart by photographs,
we have made so much life to give away,
our generous faces must outlast us!
The shadows of that richness look over
my shoulder as I pick up a postcard
with a bent pin through it. Earliest yellow leaves
are appearing on the plane trees in the square –
the playground of maturity shall bury them.

Two friends high on death – what can I say to you,
not having experienced the mystery
which choked you? Nothing of the ordinariness
which lives in words and pictures trained you
for such priesthood. You are nowhere
in the evening light: what I see instead
are two white presences, playing with life,
smiling and letting it go without reproach.

Talking to You Afterwards

Does my voice sound strange? I am sitting
On a flat-roofed beach house watching lorikeets
Flip among the scribble-gums and banksias.

When I sat here last I was writing my *Exequy*,
Yet your death seems hardly further off. The wards
Of the world have none of the authority of an end.

If I wish to speak to you I shouldn't use verse:
Instead, our quarrel-words, those blisters between
Silences in the kitchen – your plainly brave

Assertion that life is improperly poisoned where
It should be hale: love, choice, the lasting
Of pleasure in days composed of chosen company,

Or, candidly, shitty luck in the people we cling to.
Bad luck lasts. I have it now as I suppose I had it
All along. I can make words baroque but not here.

Last evening I saw from the top of Mount Tinbeerwah
(How you would have hated that name if you'd heard it)
A plain of lakes and clearances and blue-green rinses,

Which spoke to me of Rubens in the National Gallery
Or even Patinir. The eyes that see into Australia
Are, after all, European eyes, even those Nationalist

Firing slits, or the big mooey pools of subsidized
Painters. It's odd that my desire to talk to you
Should be so heart-rending in this gratuitous exile.

You believed in my talent – at least, that I had as much
As anyone of a commodity you thought puerile
Beside the pain of prose. We exchanged so few letters

Being together so much. We both knew Chekhov on marriage.
The unforgivable words are somewhere in a frozen space
Of limbo. I will swallow all of them in penance.

That's a grovel. Better to entertain your lover with sketches
And gossip in a letter and be ever-ripe for death.
You loved Carrington as you could never love yourself.

I think I am coming within earshot. Each night
I dream comic improvements on death – 'Still alive
In Catatonia', but that's no laughing matter!

Perhaps I had Australia in me and you thought
Its dreadful health was your appointed accuser –
The Adversary assumes strange shapes and accents.

And I know, squinting at a meat-eating bird
Attempting an approach to a tit-bit close to me,
That our predatoriness is shut down only by death,

And that there are no second chances in a universe
Which must get on with the business of living,
With only children for friends and memories of love.

But you are luckier than me, not having to shine
When you are called to the party of the world. The betrayals
Are garrulous and here comes death as talkative as ever.

Pope's Carnations Knew Him

But they knew they were on duty, replacing
the Rose of Sharon and the lilies of the field
for a gardener who never put a foot wrong.

It was their duty to rhyme in colour,
to repeat their reds and pinks and shield
the English rose with their Italianate chiming.

He had such a way with the symmetry
of petals, he could make a flower yield
an epic from its one-day siege. His rows

of blooms had their grotesques but they
took the place of music. They bowed, they kneeled,
they curtseyed, and so stood up for prosody.

No wonder Smart learned from their expansive
hearts that they loved the ordered, the well-heeled
and ornate, the little poet with the giant stride.

Each gossipy morning he sniffed their centres
and they saw him: the lines of paradise revealed.
God make gardeners better nomenclators.

Landscape with Orpheus

'Man lebt nur einmal, dies sei dir genug.'

It was as if the film had stuck, he was always
Back at the point where he moved up the latch
And stood facing down the street, aware of
The cicadas turning themselves on in both tall
And dumpy trees: what he saw was limited
But included lakes of dirt-in-asphalt
Before his feet, the unfortunate slug about
To cross the pavement with no more instinctive
Knowledge of its danger than he had of the sun
Perhaps on his neck, and of course always
The Dutchman's Pipe flowers he never failed
To notice, their purple mouthpieces like Disney
Saxophones, edible, sexual and howling for the dead.

It would take a lifetime to make it to the ferry,
A sunstroke's distance amid pavilioned leaves
And so desirable an ending. Well, there was a life
To spend and this was time, the softest element,
Like sap from poinsettia leaves, the milky pus
Of dreams – Eyes stood on tiptoes in those hedges,
So perhaps he should begin. It was late and it was early
In his sorrow and he had the world's tunes to play
And a landscape of peace and obsession there –
To see it all stretched out and hardly a step taken,
Such was the gift of time, walking down to the ferry
With love to come and snake-bite and the bitches flying
As calm as tapestry, in light-soaked Poussin shades.

Praise of his bloodstream flowed on then in sounds.
That this untrained imagination out of mercantile
Forebears should be Emperor of Cadences didn't surprise,
Don't we all know we are immaculate in our dress
Of self, and the twenty billion succinct souls
Hanging on God are just light in the distance
By which pilgrim feet find tracks to follow,
And that this fold of fact would undo and show
A hidden nothing if we blinked? The place of the ordinary
Is on the throne: save afternoons for judgement
And every morning for our table music. Could he have
Passed the big house with the haunted windows
And nipple-pointed fence, he had hardly moved?

But the stickiness underfoot was disquieting,
Perhaps the land was Avernus, with those
Bamboo raggednesses above the fence and the pale smell
Of warm tar on the air. Through fur of sugar-grass
He saw the river and all remote existence
Sculling across the darkened tide. What blew in his face
Were words, those he would speak in love and those
Which fattened on betrayal. The words for death
Were still unknown and yet he knew they sought him
On the street. A wind of big mothers mixing drinks
Caught him suddenly with laughter. What if he got
To the wharf, what if the ferry with a Lady's Name
Were there? He sang, in case, 'Goodnight, deceiving world!'

The cicadas stopped. Silence grew into a theatre
With everybody watching. According to the small print,
When love has failed to come you choose your end
By divination. Child or old man, now is the hour
And memory's prevarication cannot last.
With final breath whisper us your Eins, Zwei, Drei.
The sun in intervention breaks the sky,
The camera is rewound and there is the old latch,
The gate, the pepperina tree, the ferry rounding
Onions Point. The future must be crowded into now,
Paradise and hell on deck. Viewed through the telescope,
The Town Hall clock shows Orpheus looking back.

FAST FORWARD

The Flock and the Star

They stepped through the gate of life,
They moved by emergency
To the exact place of delight
There by the instinct tree.

Palmer stood them in gold
And Blake invented truth
To supplement their world,
A prison without a roof.

They are the people we know
We have been or will become:
To see them best you draw
Night and a star from the sun.

They huddle because they have no
Purpose and yet are alive.
Perhaps the beauty they see
Is why they are a tribe.

Take to this picture, God,
Consider the thing you are—
The unguideable flock,
The painstaking star.

Doll's House

Against the haunting of our cats,
Shy raids by children visiting, it stays
As truthful as the willow flats
Which blocked her days.

Its owner slammed the door and fled
Like Nora to the liberal hinterland.
What could resite that jostled bed?
No grown-up hand.

The miniature hoover lies
Brim-full of dust, the chest-of-drawers gapes;
On holidays a sobbing tries
To fluff the drapes.

And now to play at house you need
Another sort of house inside your head
Where duty states you soothe and feed
The plastic dead.

Her children have outgrown it too,
But do they hear the twisting of the key,
Entail their ruined space in lieu
Of charity?

Love, orderer of dolls and towns,
Has Lilliputianized the scale of pain,
So the wide adult eye looks down,
Bereaved again

Of esperance, the childhood flush,
And has no passage into afternoons
But through diminished doors and hush
Of darkened rooms.

A Guide to the Gods

You must recall that here they are intense,
Our gods. Each corner shop may need oblations
So the genius rests content. Kick a dog turd
Leftways to the gutter, but only if it be
Dry and crumbling. Every third display of okra
On the footpath must be stolen from—one finger
Will suffice. Touch your collar points when
Passing electricity showrooms, for there
The ghost of light supports a goddess
Veiled in wrath. Parades of the holy mad
Transferring parcels should be followed
(But judiciously). Bag women and drunks
Have been identified as Furies, but I
Do not wholly credit this. Hurry home before
The postman if you see him near your door:
That letter threatening a visit will not come.
Parse the shorter sentences in Health Food Stores,
Their higher prices are most magical.
Believe me, burst water mains may be
Oracular, but every man of sense resists
Coercion. When they wish to speak to us
The Gods behave with plainness and with modesty.
Next time I'll tell you about Zeus
Haephestos, Artemis and other probabilities,
But that is fiction and not upon our scale.

Dejection: An Ode

The oven door being opened is the start of
the last movement of Rachmaninov's Second Symphony—
the bathroom window pushed up
is the orchestra in the recitative
of the Countess's big aria in *Figaro*, Act Three.
Catch the conspiracy, when mundane action
borrows heart from happenings. We are surrounded
by such leaking categories the only consequence
is melancholy. Hear the tramp of trochees
as the poet, filming his own university,
gets everything right since Plato. What faith in paper
and the marks we make with stencils
when a great assurance settles into cantos.
The Dark Lady was no more than the blackness of his ink
say those whose girl friends are readier than Shakespeare's.
Just turn the mind off for a moment
to let the inner silence flow into itself—
this is the beauty of dejection, as if our unimaginable death
were free of the collapse of heart and liver,
its faultless shape some sort of architecture,
an aphorism fleeing its own words.
Betrayal goes so far back there's no point in
putting it in poems. I see beyond the pyramid
of faces to strong monosyllables—faith, hope and love—
charitable in halcyon's memory, fine days
upon the water and weed round the propeller.
Now all the theses out of dehydration
swarm upon my lids: I was never brave
yet half an empire comes into my room

to settle honey on my mind. Last night
I quarrelled with some friends on politics,
sillier than seeing ghosts, and now this neuro-pad
is dirging for Armenia. Despair's the one
with the chewy centre, you can take your pick.
I listened to misanthropy and had
the record straight. The woman in white,
the lady with the special presents of mind,
may now be on the phone from out of town
just to keep in touch. Think, she usually tells me,
of Coleridge and days in record shops
and all those 'likes' that love is like,
a settlement to put our world in place.
What has the truth done to our children's room?
The toys are scattered, the pillow damp with crying,
chiefly the light is poor and no-one comes
all afternoon: *Meermädchen* of the swamp of mind.
I kept my father waiting, he will know
that the disc, long-playing for however, ends
in sounds of surface, of the hinge and wind,
an average door, a tree against the pane.

To Himself

A Working from Leopardi

My exhausted heart
It is time for you to rest.
The final deceit is over, the one
I thought would last for ever.
It is dead, this love is dead
and I am content that with it
dies all hope of fond illusions
and any real desire to harbour them.
Rest now forever, heart,
you have worked too hard,
your every movement comes to nothing
and the earth which moves beneath you
is not worth sighing for.
Bitterness and emptiness compose our world,
there is nothing else; our life is made of mud.
Heart, be quietened now,
you have found your last despair.
To human kind fate has allocated
only dying: scorn Nature then,
the brutal power which rules for misery,
and the vanity of everything that is.

Going to Parties

For Philip Larkin

Truth to experience, to the sombre facts,
    We all believe in;
That men get overtaken by their acts,
That the randy and highminded both inherit
Space enough for morals to conceive in
    And prove the pitch of merit;
Such insight hangs upon the scraping pen
Of the deep-browed author writing after ten.

But there behind him, if he chose to look,
    The ranks of those
Whose sheerest now is always in a book
Are closing; yes, he's broken up some ground;
It lies about in other people's prose,
    Great graces that abound—
Meanwhile, incorrigibly, people seem
To write their own existence from a dream.

Perhaps it makes him think of earlier days
    When parties beckoned,
Quartz studs glittering in a bank of clays,
And he'd set out, though apprehensive,
Hoping this time to come in first, not second,
    Ready to really live,
Only to find that life which offers chances
Ignores the sitters-out and picks the dancers.

Yet he got something there. How to enjoy
    Expansive moments,

How it must stun the gods to be a boy
Who will not bear the cup, how unasked
Guests act prosecution and defence
    (Who was the man in the mask?)
And how exhilarating when alone
To know those dandies walk on stilts of bone.

THE AUTOMATIC ORACLE

A Sour Decade

These are the years which furnish no repentance
Though seamed with sore regret:
So much would selflessly be done and yet
Print no true sentence.

That grief sits down in books but is no writer
Must be the just rebuke,
And every lightless evening proves a fluke
The one grown brighter.

A careless management of things, they call it
Who pose for God or Fate
The purpose of the Infinite and Great
And here install it.

These decades, all the decimals of feeling,
Are pressing on our schemes.
On childhood walls, on corridors of dreams,
The paint is peeling.

Throw the Book at Them

Where do we go to live? We're born ticking
on the page and from the first disclosure on
we sense that time is useless without fear.
So here must gather all those claques of fact
we make good use of—and what are they
but words? Imagine the tight nucleus we know
is true inheritance: we find nothing more
to do with it than turn it back to chaos.
Proust could get ten thousand lines from
one night at a party and Robert Browning
knew he was in love only when he found he'd
said so on the page. How Elizabeth
loved his profile when it hovered over her
in trochees. Personification's special dangers
outweighed Daddy's growlings and the bladder
weakness of poor Flush. Rochefoucauld
spoiled things with his fully-frontal maxim:
it's all much cooler really, exile under cypresses
and chatting at the well, but never far
from the cherished self-immersing diaries—
no matter how fast they fill, white paper presses
on the eyes of nightmare and the black dog
barks defensively. There are mornings
in the bathroom when a wonky razor seems
pons asinorum of responsibility,
but don't despair, a brush with life's not final
till it's found a way to do the rope-trick
with dependent clauses. Dying's a book
with uncut pages; the pentel scurries and the tea

grows cold, and back in London a publisher
announces a burnished tome on Tuscany.
To get through life, just join the dots up, they
may prove a subcutaneous punctuation.
Today in Rouen there is an Avenue
Gustave Flaubert, but nothing spoils the stillness
at his desk. The DPP has all he needs
to start the trial—the boys in blue, the talkative
punk witnesses slurping from chipped cups.
The rules remain: you are the books you write.

The Rest on the Flight

The painted pale projectile moves and seems
Hardly to move to those inside its tide
Of twilight, as the close alliterative
Miles are ticked off charts of cloud and ocean
And still the pilgrim's face is held to sun
And still his stomach turns. A comb of words
Runs through his strands of thought continually,
Reminding him of God and lunch, of dust
At the end of day discountenancing shoes,
Of mango trees and winds in March. These props
Are human, more so than the glittering sprays
Of alcohol, the swimming-pools of in-
flight movies, or reminiscences of men
Returning to the Gulf. Packed into fear
With splendidly unlikely comrades, he
Out-herods Herod in this great escape
And relishes the massacre. Calling
The stewardess and asking for another
Miniature, he relaxes momentarily,
Is able even to risk formal scansion,
Seeming in this nowhere to stand up
Alone for seriousness, and yet frivol
In uncertainty—caparisoned
In blank verse in the blanker sky, his wings
Take him on to no place just to make
It plain to rulers of nativity
That godhead starts at home. Bring another
Whisky to the caravanserai—

At thirty thousand feet all solemn words
Are juggled out of sentence by the air,
What bubbles up is terror in its handy shape,
Heard through the headset as the ghost of hope—
Now you can write the history of the world,
Soon the little plates of Pentecost
Will be brought round accompanied by a tray
Of heated napkins, and the nose will dip
Towards the phosphor of a city; you're
Back once more to merchandising truth
Under wings of excellence, a miracle
Which Boeings make from immanence of sky.

And No Help Came

Where would you look for blessing who are caught
In published acres of millennia
By ravishments of salt and raucous saints
Or janissaries drilling a Big Bang?
The parish of the poor you'd seek, far from
The high grandstands of words and notes and paints.

And when you drove your flagged and honking jeep
Among the huts of starving, brutalized
Dependents, you might chance to hear them playing
Sentimental songs of flowers and moons
Chiefly to keep them safe from art, whose gods
Build palaces adorned with scenes of flaying.

Pontormo's Sister

The world's face is a woman's
who died early, the smoothnesses of life
waiting on a ruled horizon—
Consider this in profile even
in my *Visitation*, the four ages of Woman
unable, like God, to be anything but themselves,
and in Mary it seems lit within,
myself there, swept by darkness.
All my people are the same person,
as every artist shows: there grows a face
as hedgerows grow, as water shapes
in droplets when it falls, as we emerge
from the doors of dreams to be ourselves.
Piero's faces never vary, did he perhaps
have a sister who died too young to marry?
That's how I found technique,
a way of bending Nature to the line
of my depression. We say at twenty
and at forty and at sixty, there are
measures and distinctions you call art—
but no, we're in the shambles
with our little sisters and our parents,
we're tied to flesh and death forever
while we live, and out of it our masters ask
'Make me Veronica, the dogs and boys
grape-picking, Jesus faltering beneath
the cross's weight.' I can paint a word
if the word is death, but what I cannot do

is show it to you
unless I wrap it in a nimbus.

O little sister dressed in death,
I have painted you in everyone
and now I beg you draw the veil
across my eyes. It is time for me
to sketch God's face, a smudge of grease
on old familiarity. This is the message
of the mannered style: God looks like
anyone who ever lived, but more so.

To Lacedaemon Did My Land Extend

The heavy spirit of ambition
tells you to write first this way,
then the next, to station envy
at the door of Nature's clubmates,
circulate among Time's franchise-takers,
simply to make the most of being here—
there is no coming back, don't sourpuss
the talent-network which is all you have.
Good advice, right feeling,
though it's well to think of standing
on a wood verandah, with the gale
flapping briefly through the canvas booms
and know just as the house lizards know
that legs of self are made for running.
Once life can sense its end,
the grinding ghost inside is what
the ego-soul most wants to let go of—
departed now the tenant who would suck his soup,
the housekeeper who moulded soap-ends
into parti-coloured balls,
fled with the breakfast post
the cashiered colonel who let you test
his regimental sword—
If these are fiction's butts
it makes no odds: life's particulars
are interchangeable at the end,
our memories written by the blood
in uproar. Judgement Day will be a raffle
or the spirit's hankerings

noted by the watchful staff—
the 'good' Russian table and the 'bad'.
                              Inside the egg
first stirrings are fatigued already:
Creation must create itself once more
to find the fire. When I was young
I drugged myself with opportunity
and so lay speechless on my bed all day
unplaiting shadows. Words which spoke to me
I locked in amber. Now I am by the water,
under vines and stars, waiting for nothing,
another glass of wine to hand, a page
cooled by turning: the inventory is short—
the ants, the kitchen light, a bat re-crossing,
a drying shirt, Doreen the Dog.

Paradis Artificiel

Barbel-cheeked and hammer-toed,
I'm scrambling up a river bank
in a landscape by Claude.

I'm not bothered by that group
of humid Muses, or Apollo's
booming cattle, his frogs with croup.

I am myself a metaphor
the painter didn't think of. I'm
the monster the readers are waiting for.

The countryside's classic,
stuffed with temples and nymphs,
glazed like boracic.

And into Arcadia, bump,
comes me. As Terry Southern said,
girls go for ghouls, hump! hump!

The music I make them hear
is genital intarsia,
kinaesthesia, or sex in the ear.

How did Europe get like this?
Look at the boring planning,
crepuscular taking the piss.

Out on a verandah the gods
are having a sundowner.
They live forever, poor sods.

Unlike the sharp-eyed fellow
who dreamed this picture up,
wetting his death-bed's pillow.

I'm off then, truffling through grass
like Nebuchadnezzar, all knees—
the artist can kiss my arse

His world's not a pretty sight,
he and his nymphs need me
to guide them through the night.

Nevertheless

Heretofore
you could use words like heretofore
without embarrassment, and catch the tail
of lyricism in some suburban garden
where words were still silver
and stoically inventive verse stayed new
through all the limits of recurring sound,
being at once proconsular
and steeped in sadness. This was a time
when needles, once a shining store,
clicked in the dusk of cottage madness
under a maidenly predestined order
like the village poplars: a sad connective
linked complicity and fate,
Calvinism and the empty grate.

Moreover
what was more emphatic tipped over
into rhetoric, itself a form from which
the cooler mind could distance its approval
if the sought exaggeration seemed
too smug: viz. the walls of oak round England
and bloodless the untrodden snow.
Words went in carriages and knew
which world was which and who was who.

Notwithstanding
such non-literary facts as one may note
with understanding when the scientists
of history and language point to verse
as the least apposite of checks on how
the language went in any chosen past:
look to the lawyers and the letter-writers,
the estate agents in their coaches,
ironfounders and top-hatted railway men.
Now all the practical romantics
called from high-walled gardens
to God in a lunette: retreat was sounded
in that melancholy long withdrawing roar.
Circumlocution for these times
was the shape of Empire and an office
where words were banked or shovelled into coffers.

Nevertheless
we never move too far from Presbyterian
small print—wireless becomes the radio,
the word processor is a crutch for brains,
glossy paper takes the images of famine.
Poetry goes on being made from sounds
and syntax though even its friends confess
the sad old thing is superannuated.
Watch, though, its spritely gait as
like a bent mosquito in it walks
on the arms of three tall women in black
to mutter envious obscenities at large—

its task is still to point incredulously
at death, a child who won't be silenced,
among the shattered images to hear
what the salt hay whispers to tide's change,
dull in the dark, to climb to bed
with all the dross of time inside its head.

The Melbourne General Cemetery

This is a territory strange
To me, not the dead's embankment
But this southern city's range
Across a watered sky, the scent
Of burning, gravity's exchange.

My kept-neat city friends, the dead
I'll never meet, seem quite at one
With me. They are, no doubt, well-read,
Their stones and mounds dry in the sun
Following rain. They read in bed

Good news which goes on being news,
Old letters held before their eyes.
What we above must sift for clues
To them is fact and no surmise,
The loss of all there is to lose

Is not a loss at all. They're back
Where heavy Nothing weighs an ounce,
Where Truth is in some distant stack
And all the clawing notions pounce
On shadows in their dawn attack.

Behold amid the left-behinds
A cautious man-amphibian:
Once groping on to shore, he finds
He breathes both elements and can
Take his chance of creeds and kinds.

Almost able now to live
In life or death, this stalker looks
At those he loves, appreciative,
And knows them pictures and the books
Of Thanatation his to give.

POSSIBLE WORLDS

Woop Woop

The backtrack Trebizond of everyone,
it is in a disc of starfish where the lakes
are Balatons and the muslin-valenced ladies
bring library books to town as if it were
no more than six weeks since their husbands died.

Here start the open-shirted young sophisticates
whose fathers took the franchise for a new
variety of Cola, the ones whose poems and whose
gossip-columns are made the more intelligently
decadent by their need to tame the capital.

Out of its famished acres come anecdotes
of men with recipes for 'cockatoo-au-vin',
of fossickers in muddy dams taming Irish tunes
on one-string fiddles—rumours started here
sell beer ten thousand miles from 'Truth To Tell'.

Juggernauts are planned to pass this very place
when six-lane highways from the Bi-Centenary
stride beside the hoardings, but the point
of all this opening-up must be our doubt
that such a site will stay to welcome us.

Although an ancient and austere referent
it is younger than the harboured megalopolis
it backs, since every journey to simplicity
is inland and the parrots dress in ever-brighter
greens and scarlets the emptier the lakes they lap.

The movie industry could not exist without it:
wasp-waisted girls are seen riding after Schumann
to the soup-tin letter-box to hear that London
wants their novels, and following riots in Europe,
amuse their company just naming its odd name.

Perhaps it has no future; we know already,
despite remoteness and the different sorts of fly,
it has suburban aspects: nobody here must wait
a day to hire his favourite video, and one of its sons
read 'The Death of Virgil' through his Sunday School.

It is full of details we agree to love—
the cat called Fortunata, the minestrone
made in milk-churns, an aunt who mounted 'Tosca'
in a shearing shed: outside town, it offers you
the peace inside your mother's mind, the need to get away.

The Ecstasy of Estuaries

It is the right time to come here visiting,
Where villagers saved suicidal whales
And sand is constituted white
Beneath blue hulls—a time of times
Precluding death and constantly ahead
Of madness. Rest here, that have no absolute.

What might rock sleep is breaking out at sea
On reefs which bear the Southern Ocean;
Up-river pelicans on posts applaud
Such widening to island esplanades,
A shallow onus of the tide, the whiting
Sketching on the bottom their own shapes.

Nothing is curable but may still be endured.
Voices wait near water for career,
The karri are as various as signatures
And people out of cars confess they find
A fantasy in being what they are,
Slaves to the ancient brightness of the sea.

A magistracy of memory condemns:
Give us your childhood reminiscences,
Fan us awake with scholarship—was that
The famous Ardath pack, the Sydney Silkie's bark,
Were we the partners of those afternoons
Which lounged about in bamboo concert-rooms?

Staunchness of land slipping into light,
Of sandbanks drying from the ebbing tide,
Opens a thinking principality—
It's always a thousand miles from where to where
And will be Sunday by the railway clock,
Apprenticeship to dying in the dark.

To scatter toast crumbs to the gulping gulls
And let the dinghy flutter on the tide,
To be reliving what was hardly lived
When years ago the boat came back at dusk,
A father and a son, strange strangers, home,
This is the storytelling of the blood.

A countryside of changes still unchanged
Where no '*vielleicht*' will travel as 'perhaps',
Remorseless movement that a wayward tune
Has challenged into permanency
This ecstasy of estuaries prepares
A tableland for time to wander in.

A Chagall Postcard

Is this the nature of all truth,
The blazing cock, the bride aloof,
The E-string cutting like a tooth,
          The night that crows?

The cock has seen the standing grain,
The bride is shrouded by her train,
The violin is strung with pain,
          A cold wind blows.

From earth to sky the cry ascends,
What breaks will threaten where it mends,
Proud lovers end as pallid friends,
          These feed on those.

Civilization and its Disney Contents

Dear Readers, I offer you this impassioned book,
or, should I say, this disquisition on culture
as impassioned as I know how to make it.

It has been so often observed that what we want
is usually to do with food or sex or comfort,
but there are no systems in printing such conclusions.

And systems are what separate us from the animals;
they are the sublimity of our reasoning, the jolt
to eye and brain of the façade of San Miniato.

Our duty is to find them where others see only
a jumble of contrivances, a slogging resonance,
or the dirt-caked misery of the way the world survives.

It will never be forgiven let alone laureated to say
that the trouble with systems is that no one system
can cover everything—to work, a system must be unified.

And so you have before you my Hellenic-Hebraic law,
the tables of which I brought down from the attic,
the universality of family trunks and secrets.

But yet, like a hidden second diary or codicil
to an unfair will, I offer you a few contrary
commonplaces further to my systematic thinking.

We are not put on earth to be happy but to ensure
The effective production of Daihatsu Hatchbacks—
not even the Japanese could want to live in Japan.

Though our lives are short, time is a terrible burden.
Masters think that slavery is necessary to their riches
and slaves know that rich men constitute God's grammar.

You must have met reverent aesthetes patting rarest icons
and have known, while biting on their exquisite food,
their incomes derive from Mail Order jugs of Charles and Di.

Nothing is too far from the grave's edge, or the curtain
slung before the fire. And all the Micky, Dopey, Bambi bits
are to keep your eyes from wandering to the dancing dials.

And yet, why not? To be serious you need a grant
or to have secured tenure. The rest is journalism.
And here's a serious documentary on the survival of the beaver.

At night cicadas mourn the beasts prepared for market.
Tuscan hills vibrate to generators and to rock-and-roll.
The majesty of the Trinity wafts past an old cesspit.

Bind up the sticks for strength. We are not Fascists.
What will they dig up afterwards of us? Donald Duck is quacking
his charges off to school. He will not tell them he has cancer.

Little Buddha

'Ich bin der Liebe treuer Stern'

To see its porcelain smile
　Is a surprise in that room
With the electronic junk,
　The albums, the morning gloom,
The empty Pils neatly piled
By the futon, the light sunk
　To a hangover of dreams
　And yet, whatever it seems,
Whether indifferent to
　Fate or expectation or
Luck, its surveillance tells you
　Love can't walk out through the door.

Unbelievers, still stung by
　The need to construct a trust,
Like to set some piece of kitsch
　In place, a Madonna, bust
Of Shakespeare, Sports Day trophy,
Anything numinous which
　Shines in the Humanist dark,
　For they are set to embark
On an unknowable sea
　And the call-sign from afar
In darkness and light is 'I
　Am love's ever-faithful star.'

You sing this and try to prove
  It by rational choosing,
By doing without the bounty
  Of high romantic losing,
Keeping instead to a love
Durable as accounting,
  Traditional as the rhyme's
  Approximated sublime,
And you let the Buddha fix
  On you its unchanging look
Outfacing digital clicks
  And the brandishing of books.

But the warp remains in the soul,
  The obscenity of faith,
The creed that runs in the blood,
  The seventy years of safe
Excess succeeding control,
A dream of desert and flood,
  Of God at the index points
  Whose gift of loving anoints
The numinous animal
  With lyrical avatars,
The lure of impersonal
  Truth, a silence of the stars.

Frogs Outside Barbischio

How reassuring to listen to frogs once more
From stagnant water in an old brick cistern
Beside olive trees run wild and the unprogrammed
Flight of a butterfly over hot fields and terraces.
One grandfather frog stays on his stick to watch
A self-tormentor return to his book to trace
His anatomy of melancholy. He's in Italy
To surprise an old hopelessness known long before.

The cosmos of frogs inside its wet-walled fort
Warbles and cavorts in the all that there is.
Wise frog rejoinders have challenged that book:
Come down to our waters so pulsingly black
And lose all your stubble of fortune and truth.
Here's art inside art, incision and sign
Of the purposeless minute outlasting its span,
Of the gloat and the plop and the stick still afloat.

River Run

There is no source, though something like a bird
distances the very distance in its hoverings
and, tugging at a twig, will mark the start.

Out of nowhere to a little gully, the bits of life
like startings-up of always crying ground
gather and roll forward to a pool.

A pool, a pearl, another pearl, a pool—
the river is arriving where the dew
dries on the early paperbarks as dust.

Every childhood has its playground kills,
the innocentest cruelty and the wet
despair which no maturer pain can quell.

A time of waterfalls, of leaps round rocks
that flash their dignity, a use for history—
our fathers went down this peculiar road.

Where the gorges start, our planners stipulate
well-fenced lookouts and well-hung flowers,
blood smears of bottlebrush and banksia.

Hard-working days of green ambition,
the river and the self are broadening
among short-lived crimes, a gaudy flap of parrots.

As suddenly as afternoon the surge becomes
a modified achievement—where love has stalled,
the four-wheel-drives churn up a path of frogs.

Crops on the shore, a dog asleep upon a cushion
and the arbour heavy with the scent of lily—
out there the water-skiers skim the farther bank.

Wide as a yawn, the slow-coach river now
bastes in itself and boils the leaves
upon its surface: it is going home.

Alluvial plains of age and aspiration
needing great engineering works and
pumping stations—the doctor checks its heart.

Is this the run-up to the Third Millennium
or a ghostly dock of dreams? Each night
we take a boat upon a different thread of delta.

There in the dark, a little distance off,
the breakage sound of ocean—we will dream here
and hope never to reach the pounding Heads.

Instead, make home and common cause
with fish heads and the floating debris
of the wharfs. The river has no start,

How could it bring us to a proper end?

Serious Drinking

It comes from wanting to be perfect.
All human pain from spite to rape
Is just a reading on the grape
And all these living counterfeits
Are for philosophers' defeats;
A discontent so undivine
Moves water one notch up to wine.
Put it away, here comes the prefect.

The sinner is paid in his own coin.
Blood is love's apotheosis
And brings the liver to cirrhosis,
The flowers of sleep which towered stand
Are the famed brandy of the damned
And Wunderkinder who begin
With champagne lights may end in gin.
A drink, lest I forget thee, Zion.

Which human host can match the Devil?
God's watery water is no use—
The anthropologists' excuse
States every known society
Makes alcohol and poetry
Which in their likenesses explore
Creation's toxic metaphor.
Sober I shake and drunk I drivel.

An Ingrate's England

It is too late for denunciation:
That the snow lingers on the sill
And that there are too many newspapers
Is the same as telling yourself
You've given this country forty years
Of your days, you're implicated
In the injustices of pronouns
And the smarter speech of sycamores.

This is the England in your flesh,
A code enduring Summer while
Tasteless birds flap at the edge of
Civilizing concrete. Some have found it
Necessary to reimagine Nature
And stop importing Wordsworth
To shame the bugles from the evening air—
You were born in not the colonies but God.

Yet the brain cannot be Gloucestershire
And vents of human hate are viewed
As old cathedrals across osiers.
The selling of the past to merchants
Of the future is a duty pleasing to
The snarling watercolourist. Prinny
Used to ride by here, and still the smoke
Of loyalist cottages drips acid rain on voices.

The trains in their arched pavilions leave
For restless destinations, their PA Systems
Fastidious with crackle; nobody
Will ask you to identify yourself
But this will lead to hell, the route
The pilgrims take—down the valleys
Of concealed renewal to the pier-theatre,
The crinkle-crankle wall, the graveyard up for sale.

Copyright Universal Pictures

An immensely gifted palaeontologist
Shard-sifter has brought his virtuoso
Teenage viola-playing daughter
To the island to join him on the dig
And so encourage her to forget the quite
Unsuitable roller-skating son of a rabbi
Now proprietor of a pineapple cannery
On a remote bayou in Cajun country.

She has already noticed the only brother
Of the schizoid Alexandrian owner
Of the Crusader Castle where they excavate
Mosaics of Pyramus and Thisbe and airborne
Ganymede, the oldest of their kind in Paphos.
He has published one book of sonnets privately
From Keele University entitled *Atlantis, Atys,*
Attica, and brought his Burt Reynolds videos.

Professor Fuori Sanguinetti, who has had to leave
Catania University hurriedly and who hopes to
Acquire some Hellenistic artefacts for a firm
Of antiquarians in the Veneto to whom his wife
Is seriously in debt, suspects that our
Loving father is not everything he seems and that
The Manager of the Phylloxenia Hotel
Is either an agent of the KGB or CIA or both.

The poet is on a deserted beach breaking open
Shells for the viola-player, telling her how the fish

When boiled made a purple dye called Murex—
'Gee, you're a bore,' she says. 'I came here to get laid.'
The little waves like Aphrodite's feet lie down
In the spume and gulls snatch wrappers from the sand—
This is the scene she said she wouldn't do nude
Which will be on the posters when the film's released.

The Professor has followed them and watches from
The dunes; above the bay a helicopter circles
While a fishing boat is anchored out of sight
Below the Rock of All the Romans. Along the road
The Manager approaches in a Pre-War Chev.
We are not shown what will become of this
And pan back to the diggings where we see
The child-god simper m the eagle's claws.

The poet has begun a sonnet and from a room
Just over his the sound of Paganini studies
Drives an alto nimbus through the evening light;
Reynolds has beaten up a man in all-night
Diner in St Louis, and the screen goes blank—
The girl and her father come into the lobby and greet
A man in a panama hat whose sweat-circles
Below his arms spread almost to his waist.

Articles of clothing catch the moon beside
The hotel swimming pool. Arpeggios of bubbles
Accompany naked limbs. A blue fish from Murano
Swims in air above Reception and trunks are loaded

On a BMW. The story will move on to Rhodes
And leave this cheap-to-film-in corner
Of the great inane. Leave, too, the unimportant
Like ourselves. Next shift, it may be Athens.

The Orchard in E-Flat

The waves are weeping vaguely. Confessional dust
Plagues the opacity of ocean and a book
Lies down at angles—scene-setting by our sons.
A god is rising from the ambient air
As though there were no griefs and nothing died
But there appeared a wholesome vanity
For us to live in: evangelizing light
Is spread before a holy picnic, goats
And men move down the isthmus to dark bells.

The numberlessness of stones is speaking for
The helplessness of people—debts, deaths and
Spoliations are a tuning of the world,
A chord of limitless additions, but
Anywhere a road leads over hills
And temperate dawns to some encumbered cabin
Where the bruise of exile turns to timeless rose.

Sequences are set by leaves, the ripplers' coven,
Even as Aeolian sounds are congregated
To pick up yells of history or the bubble-breath
Of dying, separate conveyances of truth,
Some convected into keyboard plausibilities
And some to concert strokes of sanity.
Evil at its console feels for carpet-slippers
Choosing the classiness of the baroque.
Surely such categories include the double.

Behind us is the deep note of the universe,
The E-Flat pedal on which time is built,
Spreading and changing, both a subtle
Growth of difference and a minimalist
Phrase, with bridges crossing it and staves
Of traffic on its tide, a broad bloodstream
To carry to the delta full mythologies.

A mother and a boy come to the orchard
To turn a cow back to its field; they see
The ducks in line-ahead among the crimson
Pointillism of the windfalls and,
Overheard by them, the everlasting anthem
Changes as injustice starts to sing—
There's wood enough within: it fires the earth,
The creatures coming home, the buried bones
And pairs of ears poised, the weeping waves.

THE CHAIR OF BABEL

Bad Dreams in Venice

Again I found you in my sleep
And you were sturdily intact,
The counsel you would always keep
Became my dream's accusing tract.

Still I dared not think your force
Might even slightly slack my guilt—
This wasn't judgement but a course
Which self not knowing itself built.

It scarcely mattered where I dreamed,
The dead can choose a rendezvous:
You knew that nothing is redeemed
By blame, yet let me conjure you.

And this was Venice where we'd walked
Full tourist fig, first man and wife
On earth, and where we'd looked and talked
Your presence could outlive your life.

But now Venetian vapours clung
To every cold and wounding word—
The spectres which we moved among
Came from the phrases I had stirred.

They could not harm you but they bit
Into whatever had not died;
However we might reason it,
Your face and mine marched side by side.

And those old harshnesses which you
Muttered to me unrestrained,
Like Venice, loved but hated too,
Were all the closeness which remained.

Bad Dreams in Naples

My mind, that privatized Maecenas,
Has struck a bargain with my penis:
I dream a violent cityscape,
My feet stuck on with sellotape.

The boys of Spacca–Napoli
Are on their bikes pursuing me,
With girlfriends perched on hot machines,
Their labia outlined by their jeans.

I'm drinking Ischian white wine,
It's someone's piss, not even mine,
And now instead of riding pillion
My head is under Hugo Williams.

Around me genitals and faces
Appear in unexpected places—
A tap I chance to stand beside
Unzips my fly and feels inside.

I know what hurts me terribly,
The jokes and lack of dignity—
That fear should show contempt as well
Indubitably smacks of hell.

Yet this is better than the tilt
Which moves the action on to guilt.
A terrified and dying man
Is seeking his estranged wife's hand.

The Manager croons, con amore,
'No credit cards, please, Professore.'
I say my poetry will pay,
He shrugs and looks the other way.

They're packing me into my shroud.
I recognize it as the cloud
Always above Vesuvius.
My soul hangs round for God to suss.

So much for transcendentalism!
All the colours of the prism
When blended make one living light.
He breaks them up to keep them bright.

Wish We Were There

It would be our garden of scents and Spitfires,
it would be our yard for exercise,
it would go on for ever (and ever),
it would, of course, be Paradise.

And be fitted like a German kitchen,
every pleasantness at eye-level,
the cats on their curly yellow cat-mat
unequivocally of the Devil.

Mother and Father in frayed straw hats
and swatches of angelic flannelette,
the nimbus of childhood spreading wider,
the milkman trying to place a bet.

Getting old would be growing younger
as the CDs turn at 78
and Haydn's No. 97
provides a coda for Beethoven's Eighth.

The pet dogs buried by the roses
should rise from the limed and clayey soil
and the Council steamroller-driver
bring belated tears to the boil.

The post come twice a day from Youville
with letters of triumphant love—
you and Joseph on the river,
you with Fyodor by the stove.

And there too Indestructible Man
would keep death lurking by each bush,
clipping and pruning tirelessly,
the old lawnmower hard to push.

The voice of friendship calling up,
can you come down today to play
so time shall not move round the dial
and after-breakfast last all day.

The macaronic airs refresh us,
taking pity on a poor linguist
till it's Pentecost and Schubert's Miller
takes his withered flowers for grist.

The end is nigh but will not happen
as tea appears on the lawn—
the synchronicity of Heaven
is owed to us for being born.

Pigeons, Gulls and Starlings

Imagine a heaven where every one of these
is known by bar codes on its wings or tail.

Where someone cares beyond importing them
into an apophthegm about survival.

Better for them to stick to their concourse
of things abutting, edges without flighting.

We like to think they clean the wounds of feeling,
the scabs which form around dependency.

It's not that they like scorpions will survive
the fire storm, just that they aren't concerned.

A philosopher might teach one how to talk
and find it walked right past philosophy.

Yet a bird could share with a philosopher
the poverty of dreaming one dream always.

The syncopation of our kindness: we
shoo them from the lawn when wood-doves land.

They can't be rare and lovable, or mime
their gratitude like hungry ducks ashore.

Come *The Last Supper* in the Park, they know
France's premier chef is named L'oiseau.

They've been with Jesus and at Venice, viz.
renowned St Gull's, St Pigeon's and St Stare's.

Pray for the sadness of intelligence,
the many lives envisaged in the one.

In Rosewell

These small, well-built and greystone Lothian houses
Seem full of sadness, ringed about by sky.
Unlike the flock of birds my presence rouses
Their dignity will wait till I go by.
Perhaps they feel that one who lives in books
Is hardly worth a turbulence of rooks.

The birds have high trees and a castled river
To underwrite their screaming senate's noise
As down the wet roads juggernauts deliver
Animals to death, and cycling boys
Pass kennels where impounded dogs and cats
Howl to the lonely lawns and council flats.

How should a writer better test self-pity
Than standing soaked outside the Miners' Club
With letters of importance for some city
And far too shy to go into the pub?
I bring my quiet burden to the post,
A lifetime's correspondence with a ghost.

The Chair of Babel

We are in the fashionable Republic of Evil
for an especially relevant conference.

My neighbour has been first on his feet
after each paper with a question.

I see from his conference entry
he has the Chair of Babel
in a taxidermist's country.

Unfortunately it's so hot
we keep the windows open and the noise
of traffic fillets every sentence.

Half of us speaks one language and half
another, though their half knows ours well
and our half's monoglot.

The official translator is a genius—
'The lady says her case is near-Hegelian'
he likes to start—

This morning my neighbour asked
'Why do Schubert's lieder hymn the sea
and fisher-folk when he had seen no stretch
of water wider than a lake?'

The translation went: 'The landlocked mind
will ever seek an amniotic . . .'

I turned my headphones on and heard
'The camera runs, the wildcat eats the hare . . .'

The noise at coffee-break is settling down
at about G below middle C, I guess.

At lunch yesterday two conferenciers
had their bags stolen by youths who rode
mopeds through the restaurant.

Case histories tend to leap from
shit and bonding to repair
ignoring counter-transference.

We are united in distrusting one old man
whose sense of humour is exaggerated.

Viz., he said, 'This reminds me of
Judge Schreber's childhood harness which only
Houdini could have masturbated in.'

I've seen one car which halted at the lights
but that was when they'd turned to green.

A Venezuelan hung around with gold
suggested we imagine suicide
as a function of God's Repo-Firm.

The conference is in a palace
with *trompe l'oeil* walls
seemingly adjacent to Arcadia.

I dream of people making love inside my body
quite unconcerned that I am watching them.

But now I know what we are here for—
it's in the Bible, that club of confidences—

A buzz of international cooperation
doubtless held hubristic somewhere else.

Stuffed melanzane and fizzy wine
are served beside old fish ponds
by the light of floating tapers.

I say to my neighbour,
daring to speak to him at last,
'Is yours a big department?'

'We have Gossip, Pentecost,
Green Vocabulary,
Eye Utterance
and Cultspeak,' he replies.

The plane to take us home
is blessed by several Cardinals
and provided by
The Cooperative Society of Ghosts.

Wittgenstein's Dream

I had taken my boat out on the fiord,
I get so dreadfully morose at five,
I went in and put Nature on my hatstand
And considered the Sinking of the Eveninglands
And laughed at what translation may contrive
And worked at mathematics and was bored.

There was fire above, the sun in its descent,
There were letters there whose words seemed scarcely cooked,
There was speech and decency and utter terror,
In twice four hundred pages just one error
In everything I ever wrote—I looked
In meaning for whatever wasn't meant.

Some amateur was killing Schubert dead,
Some of the pains the English force on me,
Somewhere with cow-bells Austria exists,
But then I saw the gods pin up their lists
But was not on them—we live stupidly
But are redeemed by what cannot be said.

Perhaps a language has been made which works,
Perhaps it's tension in the cinema,
Perhaps 'perhaps' is an inventive word,
A sort of self-intending thing, a bird,
A problem for an architect, a star,
A plan to save Vienna from the Turks.

After dinner I read myself to sleep,
After which I dreamt the Eastern Front
After an exchange of howitzers,
The Angel of Death was taking what was hers,
The finger missed me but the guns still grunt
The syntax of the real, the rules they keep.

And then I woke in my own corner bed
And turned away and cried into the wall
And cursed the world which Mozart had to leave.
I heard a voice which told me not to grieve,
I heard myself. 'Tell them', I said to all,
'I've had a wonderful life. I'm dead.'

Listening to Shakespeare

I was at school with him
that Will Shakespeare,
carved his name on his desk,
pissed on it to make it shine,
edited a magazine called *Nova*
the name of our river spelled backwards—
he said we should always remember
that words were the way you told lies
and got out of a walloping—
he got us to compare our penises
and said one boy's was Small Latin
and another one's Less Greek,
he kept us entertained with faces
and wrote endless essays
when he wasn't courting.

When he went to London
I was really sorry. Or was it Lancashire?
Anyway we heard of him in London,
then his Dad got into trouble about church
and his Old Woman sulked at home
and we had several discontented winters.
One day I met him in the High Street,
he seemed a bit furtive,
said the chap loitering on the corner
was a government spy,
'haven't I got trouble enough with Coriolanus?'
I loved his stories from the classics
but it only made him gloomy,

‘You know what Marston told me,
all Penelope did in Ulysses’ absence
was fill Ithaca full of moths—
why come back when the moths at home
are never going to change to butterflies?’
I showed him a review in the local paper,
‘Stratford author’s sour-note sonnets’.
He wasn’t interested and talked
about the price of real estate.

But he was big in London,
you heard about it even here.
And all the time he bought up property
and made himself a gentleman
like his father had tried but failed to do.
Then he came home, old and tired,
saying if life’s race were run from eleven to ninety
he was at the ninety end
though all of forty-eight.
Once at an Open Day he said mysteriously
‘Congratulations, you have just invented
a new art form—let’s call it Local History
and hurry it along to Heritage.’

We listened when he talked to us.
I used to love his high haranguing
but it died away. He died too,
quite suddenly. Managed a good tomb
before the altar and no digging-up

and stowing in the ossuary. I've kept a note
he passed me under the desk once
during a long grammar lesson.
'No man may know a neighbour closer
than his own defeat. The unfolding star
calls up the shepherd. Soon there'll be
nothing of the world to listen to.'

A Tour of the City

In the tenth week of the siege
I discovered I could triplicate my limbs
and looked bemusedly at my six arms
lying parallel in the bath.

The enemy had built a tower
which out-topped our walls and thus they must soon
move against us. Sieges, of course,
had long since ceased to happen
but fear of dying musked the air,
a seriousness glossed by caricature.

Suddenly I could not bear to look,
the gods were walking by our gates,
star-poultices against their eyes
to stem the glare of our carnality.

The body can't hold ecstasy:
I clasped them to me
knowing they were exactly what they seemed,
the huge and radiant intercessors
whom books and nerves have sanctified
in every generation—and the joy
of talking with them raised the siege,
I could tell my friends we were beloved,
these ancient specialists would contrive
an exile for us, not a final death.

The timed naturalness of their skin,
enjambment of intensity and fate,

could co-exist with tractable delight—
their conversation was of Irish priests
who baptised long cigars, their choruses
a clawback from Euripides
and chocolate nightingales.
I cried for sheer simplicity
as though I took an everlasting heart
from my long-buried mother. The siege was time
and would be brought again but they would know
a passage through the vines, a blood funicular.

They had the dryness of encyclopaedias,
a wide disclaimer like a page which opens
on a saffron lake with fish-nets drying
and a castle lapped by water; their halcyon
was the opposite of miracles,
the first hours of a holiday, your mouth
finding its own way to hot bagels,
ahead a terrace lunch, a via dolorosa
lined with moulting figs. The blurred gods
were the first tourists and true pathfinders—
it is hilarious to meet them, Lady Hesters
under veils of lightning, translating
the epodes of a Montenegrin shepherd.

The whole world was their city and they took
my hand and led me to the parapet
and showed me which great doors were closed,
what cupboards Bluebeard kept the keys of

and which departing buses knew the road.
In my bath two arms now seemed enough,
the skylight garlanded the sun—outside
the city simmered and the gods were gone,
back to the paper of their ecstasy.

The Cartrac Quatrains

The deaf man at the ranting rail
Thought Ulysses by the mast a liar
To dare the supernatural lewd
Yet give it flesh in which to dwell.

They'd travelled troubled miles through maps
On nothing more than hope and spam.
From figurehead to galley rats
The whole crew sought a landward star.

The Chief would tell their chancy saga
To any girl, call it a gas—
King's daughter, sorceress or diva,
His salty words made each one avid.

They'd passed beyond the sucking pool,
The chute of soot, the strangling loop,
They'd trembled at the giant's step
And put baits out for Circe's pets.

Up at the helm, an unmoved slob
Swilled his mouth with heavy Bols
And from the sleep of tainted pork
Devils came, a spectral crop.

Philosophers had taught them time
Is infinite, that skies emit
Ill luck alone and in the trap
Of hope endurance plays its part.

And now they sulked in Venus' cart
Along some star-directed track,
The sea their home, a final coma
Where death and memory run amok.

MILLENNIAL FABLES

The Approach Road

They didn't tell you how you were to go,
Only that you must start and having started
Should keep in mind the big road up ahead,
That what you swore to do as you departed
Would be forgotten in the contraflow
Of signs you followed, skirmishes you led
While wilful herds went slow and insects darted.

The twilight thickens and the darkening road
Appears to narrow through its banks of green;
The clouds and trees have fossilized together
As if they wouldn't let the car between—
Here are the megaliths the route-map showed,
The dried-up lake, the starveling moor of heather,
Yourself the image on the startled screen.

World Poetry Conference Welcome Poem

Brothers and sisters, whether joined or singlish,
        We bring you greetings from our lovely land—
Everything will be exposed in English
        so delegates and lovers understand.

We are in no doubt publishers of Man
        and Man has thieved the spark which fires the clay,
so welcome everyone and sparkle soon
        and we will have for certain a nice day.

Our country has great dams and several sorts
        of mentionable fruit—what has yours?
Our friendly poems like to go in shorts
        and your hotel will have the cricket scores.

What do we need with Scuds and Dreadnothings
        when smart's the word for pantoums and haiku?
Our Minister has made war so disgusting
        that we love peace and poetry like you.

We say our neighbours are the sun and moon
        and we make love to ocean with our feet.
We hope that you will couple with us soon
        to join our satisfactory élite.

Aesop's Dressing Gown

The spillings on lapels and cuffs, according
to his fellow queuers at the bathroom door,
were sloppy eggs and greedy second helpings,
but he knew better—they were what healthy
overreachers of commercial mornings
make of conscience: he would study them
and see the fox and grapes, the farmyard shapes
these others never could construe. He fought
consensus with his smelly feet; if truth
came up as lumps it meant that lice
were called again to be inquisitors—
meanwhile that gravy stain should be
a pond for pompous frogs to trumpet in;
a crumb might make King Log but certainly
he'd blown his nose down one sleeve as King Stork.

What may an underdog perform if not
squeeze fables from occlusions of his brow?
Since Everyman is unreformable
he must be entertained with heavyweight
impactions of his own imagination.
Aesop set out for his appointment at
the portraitist's in his coat of many cringes,
more bad breakfasts than Achilles' shield
had ships and warriors, better shadows there
than death knew how to frame for underlings—
he might be thought when brash posterity

circuited the gallery some old
and grave retainer with a book, rather than
what he knew he was, a hired explainer
of the gods' obtuseness to the gods.

Winckelmann at the Harbourside

I tell the man
standing by his sloop
we come down from the North
to get away from hope

Water oils around its keel—
to spit into the wake
won't change anything,
what's classic
is repetitively new

History, from Herodotus
to the boy at the *Pensione Mercurio*
is infinite desire
mocked by timeless need

Berenson Spots a Lotto

It takes me back to my beleaguered youth,
Chiming across an Italy where carts
Rocked down dirt roads and crones without a tooth
Unlocked the doors of chapels, and bleeding hearts
On banners, flung aside, revealed an altarpiece
Whose dim and long-dead donor thought to win
A sort of immortality, his Fleece
Of Gold in Heaven, sitting painted in
A flock Annunciation or some ghetto
Holy Family. Year after year I roamed
The provinces from Como to Loreto,
But this was just the fieldwork: I had homed
In on the big boys from the start and knew
That not just railway magnates but the scholars
Wanted certainties, the only true
Account of Europe, and beyond the dollars
A secret map of Christianity
Waited projection by a doubting Jew.
So these my lonely forays were for me
And for my conscience: I felt the world askew
But told it straight: as Burckhardt was the first
To show, the art of Europe's a crusade
And universal culture is a thirst
In conquerors whose vanities have made
Our palaces and charnel houses grow—
The story must be written, heroes found
Masaccio, Piero, Michelangelo,
A triumph set to pass its native ground
And bear the Western spirit into space,

With me its true evangelist, the one
Who'll say authoritatively a face
Is duly a Farnese, but not shun
The central mystery, the major-key
Colossi, men whose grandeur connoisseurs
Can only blink at—thus it falls to me
To play commander, wear the holy spurs.
And, yes, you've heard my word's corrupt, my voice
In grading minor masters built my villa,
And somebody has rhymed me á la Joyce,
A prophet, *Teste David cum Sibylla.*
I'm the greatest art expert the world's ever seen,
I make attributions for Joseph Duveen,
From tycoons and bankers I draw a fat fee,
So here's to Vecelli and Buonarroti.
The grandeur falls away and Duveen's dead,
And Europe sinks once more into Avernus.
It's good in one's old age to leave one's bed
And young again to stalk such joys as burn us,
The glorious anarchy of what we love,
All stupid scales of value tossed aside
So that a Dosso Dossi seems above
A Titian and we'd die to prove our pride
In Credi or Melozzo: exhausted now
With rugs about my knees, in a wheelchair,
On this my final pilgrimage, I vow
To praise the greatness of that inner air
Which blows about the spirit: they said I'd find
The cutest Visitation in this glum

And barrel-chested church, so, wined and dined,
I'm here and have to laugh—it seems I've come
Full circle to the proving-ground of youth:
I'm bang in front of something I adored
When as a thrusting expert seeking truth
I first encountered it: the Virgin bored,
The Baptist's mother a strange shaft of blue
And two dogs fighting round their feet, the limbs
Half spastic but in everything a hue
Collated from the spectrum's antonyms—
Lorenzo Lotto, my first darling, I
Assigned you half a page in my big book
But more than ten years seeking-out—are we
Then reconciled—you with your beaky look,
Your death's pre-echo and me at the gates
Of terror and oblivion? Your luck
Was to be provincial in the Papal States,
Not smart enough for Venice where they suck
Up gold from mud and splash it on the stars—
You worked a density that fashion loathed
And paid the price of it, your avatars
The quirky poses, matrons overclothed
And cats astounded by angelic draughts.
Old friend, I'm with you now, I've done with fame
If never quite with money—Arts and Crafts
I leave to Night School mumblers and the same
For those grand galleries and owners—let
Them examine sizes, pigments, drapes, x-rays
I'll give a provenance in a minute

They won't unseat—and Lotto, our last days
Can be the sweetest; you in the warm wind
From the Adriatic fixing the bizarre
With daily habits; me, more sinning than sinned
Against, and princely in a chauffeured car,
Doing my lap of honour coast to coast,
Detesting Modern Art, unpenitent
Of theft or fraud, the last admiring ghost
Of Europe's genius, all passion spent.

DRAGONS IN THEIR PLEASANT PALACES

Kings and Messengers

Someone, leaning out, said Look it's what
We call the Learning Curve and bang the freight
Shifted in the back and whiffs of hot
Macadam wafted in: I saw my chance
And shouted at them all, No need to wait,
A dream's imagination's ambulance.

That's when the Kafka rules took over—we
Ate aphorisms like porcini, wrote
Our paradoxes as love-letters, free
In their compulsive intellect of all
Simplicity, and what we chose to quote
Was back-street grovelling by a prodigal.

The rushing messengers disowned their kings
But relished livery: they had the Arts
For ukase, scams and heists and stings
To keep them modern, and appraising thoughts
Of sex and synergy, their counterparts
Successive saviours at besieged airports.

Hardy, 1913

When she he mourned had guided him beside
The cliffs and gates of courtship long ago
And ghost-like by the sea which howled below
Her form had surged and eddied with the tide,

When birds whose names both knew still multiplied
In makeshift air around, and counterflow
Of cloud and leaf-light once more set aglow
Her cheeks and nurtured his defensive pride,

He came back to his desk and framed in words
Those elegies in which his world lay wrecked,
His New Year songsters changed to mangled birds,

And still to show him what life cedes to art
Remorse kept house with her safe in his heart,
Her pets all killed or dead from his neglect.

Old Goldfields, Maryborough

A terror made for midday,
they had walked in galleries beneath our feet
through tinted naves of clays and quartz
five miles and back to Maryborough
and hardby vents and blowholes seen the pulleys
raising ore through Roman arches
and the spacious graveyards fit for those
who never could feel safe in only air.
And now stout Hattie, energy's own dog,
is on the wrong side of the underworld
scouting at the creek's torn barbican
to sniff to life the latest of lost worlds.
Down such a rabbit hole
the Nineteenth Century lured our grandfathers
and great-grandfathers—
gold made sense
of leaving home, entitled all who hate themselves
to test the power of fortune: impervious gold
was a gem in destiny, and all along
a parliamentary Nature was on hand
to clean the mess up. For fifty years
the earth lay gashed by hopefulness and built
a sort of easily assembled Babylon
for these new-minted Gods—today
some sixty souls are forum for the trumpet
of its silent Judge.
When Hattie's rambles
take her to the mullock heaps, she skirts
a fossicker with detector and soft hat

looking for the fillings in this skull.
                                        The landscape now
is featureless as scar tissue
though scrub revives wherever water rides
and ghosts of acid-fingered men
hover as hurt roses or the plums
which fall before the sun has sugared them.

The Western Canoe

We are all in it together, paddling downstream
as in that clip from *Sanders of the River*
but with no one around to shout 'Come on Balliol!'

Undoubtedly here's history in the Steiner sense,
so late into creativity that commentary
gets the prizes, the sexy must of lecturing.

And Bloom's great gun booms heartily
making up for all those snubs, and if he seems
a kosher butcher, at least he's not the Theory Fairy.

In truth, this is a well-equipped canoe,
brother to the Gulf War one, and as attrition
weakens Gibbon, the crew is laser-limning history.

Films are shown on board: *Sophocles' National Service*,
Pico and Vico at the Deux Magots,
Alkan the Alien—but what's so terribly difficult

is starting up afresh. How did they do it, Emily
and friends, out there in the sticks, knowing that a gang
of snobs and clerics had turned the signposts round?

Bliss in that dawn! And if our dawns are chemical
some things never change—a Suburban Sports Reporter
enjoys the engine capacity of a Dickens.

As the canoe beats the rapids to enter the vast
waters of the Eco Pool, drums are calling
for a TV war replete with ice and orphans.

Dangers of shoals and drifting debris, reading habits
of electronic shoppers—and for the academically-inclined
dropping buoys off in The Swamp of Likenesses.

It reminds us of Maurice Bowra cruising the Aegean—
Daphnis and Chloe country for the educated—
and what are our lives but a narrative of metaphor?

Approaching us, a war canoe half The Lady Murasaki,
half state-of-the-art modem, and in a dream
the 'Waratah' still on her maiden voyage.

Hot in headphones, brushing off the monkeys,
Mr Kurtz hears what the King of Brobdingnag
told Gulliver. He'll reappear upriver.

Collateral Damage

'Beethoven was an ugly man, short of stature, with a pock-marked face cut by blunt (or clumsily-guided) razors, and in his late years with a body-odour strong enough to empty the largest table at any of his favourite Viennese restaurants.' John Deathridge, *TLS*

I see it this way, Mr Beetfield,
you can't do anything that's true pin-point,
there's always one shot goes astray
and some poor thing that got in range
has to be apologised for when damage
is assessed, with all the pictures in.

And minims, liver-spots on God's back-of-hands,
are disappointment's fine embellishment:
the café empties like a concert hall
at such reiteration, and that wretched frame
the pianoforte's a mechanical lyre
for each new Orpheus with attitude.

Exactitude, as I insisted, Mr Beetharvest,
has its price. I mean any farmer knows
breeding is selection and half a herd
can feel the fall-out. That loaves and fishes draught,
well, you couldn't do it if you had to say
No to factory farming. God gives the means.

Music is prosthesis, the jutting-out of truth
beyond performers' fingers.
Because it makes no difference when we're dead
the extraordinary must be fashioned now,

the impossible made sane ambition
and the body a crucifixion of the mind.

It's as if we're in two parts, Mr Beetsugar,
like that guy Montaigne wrote—imagination
puffs us up and reality deflates us.
When the vet said this won't be a healthy calf,
if I'd believed him I'd have lost
a square-eyed runt became my best milk-giver.

The bombardment lingers in the air
as octaves, and the awful pain of deafness
still resonates above the stave.
Looked at another way, a youthful virtuoso
tells his mistress he mustn't marry
having already composed her rejection of his love.

I'm an amateur of ballistics, Mr Beetweevil,
and I don't value megadeath or even
cluster bombs and shrapnel. The point of God
is perfect aiming, something we can't do
on earth. And yet it seems our progress,
as we call it, comes from near-misses.

Darkness visible—perhaps, or
silence audible—or crowding
immeasurability in a phrase.
The silent piano weeps on earth—
time rots in Heaven, ignoring
the *fingerfertigkeit* of angels.

The Lion of Antonello da Messina

My lion tells me
that the word can kill and will do so
without warning. Together we have
house-trained terror till it's fit
to undertake a miracle for Science.
The underworld of things is Paradise,
the sun in stained-glass portholes made
to adore the laws of its dismantling
and all the books which must be studied
if Creation is to stay on course—
witness then the sheer assemblage
of this quiet; has any other sainted cell
so radiant a cross-section?
Without my lion nothing would connect,
he is the way imagination went
while God was still explaining it.
Antonello can't domesticate
my cauldron of a mind and so
he tidies everything and has the lion state
Jerome is king of thinking beasts.
But to get the entire world into
so small a painting is more than skill,
it adds up to theology.
Of all the lions I've had, this beast
of Antonello's is the most complete;
he lays his muzzle in my lap
as if he knows it is a fearful thing
to fall into the hands of the living god.

The Pines of Rome

(For Katherine & Royston)

As ghosts of old legionaries, or the upright
farmers of that unbelievable republic,
the pines entail their roots among the rubble
        of baroque and modern Rome.

Out by the catacombs they essay a contradiction,
clattering their chariot-blade branches to deny
the Christian peace, the tourist's easy frisson,
        a long transfiguration.

Look away from Agnes and the bird-blind martyrs,
the sheep of God's amnesia, the holy city
never built, to the last flag of paganism
        flying in mosaic.

Then say the pines, though we are Papal like the chill
water of the aqueducts, refreshment from a state
divinity, we know that when they tombed the martyrs
        they ambushed them with joy.

Rome is all in bad taste and we are no exception
is their motto. Small wonder that Respighi, 'the last Roman',
adds recorded nightingales to his score *The Pines*
        of the Janiculum.

And the scent of pines as we dine at night
among the tethered goats and the Egyptian waiters
is a promise that everything stays forever foreign
        which settles down in Rome.

Therefore I nominate a Roman pine to
stand above my slab, and order a mosaic
of something small and scaly to represent
my soul on its last journey.

The Cocks of Campagnatico

The heart grown old can't fake its scholarship
And won't essay that glib insightfulness
Which once it made a moral landscape from:
This village, half its human figures and
Its cats and dogs enthroned in windless sleep.
Law's brutal now—a German bus deep-parked,
A gang of no-ones-in-particular
Kicking to death a pigeon—how may they be mapped?

Only within the self can scales be hung.
Ignore mere detail says the ageing conscience,
Encourage emblems any mind can hail.
And so the roosters of the valley stir
As if to answer such a challenge, though
They're late, their tubs of sun already full,
And beautifully redundant to themselves
Propose and repropose the Resurrection.

A Lament

In valleys where winds meet,
in silences of chambers
untouched by the sun,
in tufa uplands and long strata
of the vanished waters,
we will find them—
our salted ancestors
in households still outflanked
by cat and ibis mummies,
the losing parts of ghostliness
not magicked now by moon or stars—
their eyes would sweep forever
super sydera, but that they have no eyes
nor ears, but only a long nothingness
imagined by the gods.

In dreams they visit us
but it is our lives which are
their prison. They made their tombs
and temples to invigilate our thoughts
and their dementia is our memory.
Though such messages are fading from us
a chemical exchange goes on—
a dynasty of prayers becomes a waterfall,
a warrior's resting place the chair
of some sand-flooded tractor.

When all the lives which ever were or ever will be
are trimmed like stone and share
stone's magical inertness
winds will still lament the strangeness
which was life and silence look to find
its birthplace in an allegoric music.

And the winds say
What did you do in the war, Daddy?
and the reply, I kept my gas mask on.
Nothing is straightforward
and the shortest distance between two points
may be the way to death,
and gravity is bounced about the rocks
by private zephyrs. The only sound now
is a lift ascending to the floors
of non-existence. They wait there for us,
our friends and lovers recognizable
as we shall be by their perfect missingness.

Dragons in their Pleasant Palaces

Where are the Science Students? Gone to Media Studies,
so why not take the Bible down and get a high
from old Isaiah? Half of what we mean by poetry
is still the rhetoric Hebrew makes in English.
Phasing in a little modern jargon—The Internet,
Pacific Rim, bi-polar wiring—and off we go
back to the full portfolio of lamentation,
the Psalmist's barefoot cries in Askalon,
the Voice of Him that cryeth in the Wilderness
and still breaks wind in Wollongong or Widnes.

The hilltop villages are plangent with goat cries
as water-carts ascend past millet-rows—
stop the bus! this coping stone's an uncle to
reluctance, and *Insh'allah*—where sparrows splash
a generation of fine mercers trained to be
the only hosts a prim cénacle knew—
here Tancred and Clorinda made the closing scene
while ravens, Hittites and black scorpions
catered to the Prophets. These stone museum lions
once were hungry mouths for Ashurbanipal.

As God Eternal joined time in his Mother
phenomena persist of dust collecting in
the sealed mechanism of a watch
and teeth come up decayed. Since figs must ripen
as they did a million years ago, eyes in
the Bible Lands dilate at searing jets

and burning rigs are pillars raised by night—
the very air has purged itself of progress—
such dragons not away on a consultancy
are making inventories of our palaces.

BOTH ENDS AGAINST THE MIDDLE

Leaving Mantua

I woke up early as I invariably do
    when I have an early train to catch –
    a dream-master has no need of clocks.

The night before I'd argued in my language
    with two Italian ladies who might have been
    happier in theirs: had I been rude or thoughtless?

One was wrong, undoubtedly, to think Shakespeare's
    works were written by the Earl of Oxford
    but they both resided in Mantua and I

Was in exile from myself, or so I told myself,
    looking at the stallions on the wall
    of the Palazao Te: 'here is for me no biding'.

And wasn't I as grossly opinionated
    about Italian painting as she on Shakespeare?
    My head hurt after a thick wine they'd been happy

To leave to me, and I'd toyed with beetroot-coloured
    strips of meat once more maintaining
    our Northern barbarism – drink ahead of food.

Struggling past the desk (I'd had the sense to settle
    the bill the night before) I pushed my case to the street
    sheeted from eave to cobbles in soup-thick mist.

Where in this Dantesque gloom might the station be?
    I knew I'd find it and that in the meantime
    I'd enjoy the sense of apprehension.

Some text-book facts were circling in my mind:
the lakes formed by the Mincio which made Mantua
the unhealthiest city in all Italy,

The midday gravitas which even bold Mantegna
found obsessively marmoreal, the grim
abutting jokes which Giulio proved sexy.

Yet the Gonzaga, as their Estense neighbours,
lived in the sun and left it up to Shakespeare
to conjure terror for us from their name.

I'd seen King Charles's pictures bought from
Mantua's sack, or what we have of them
after Cromwell sold them off—I'd followed

A troop of noisy children just to view
the Pisanello frescoes in the Reggia.
I'd been in Mantua only once before,

And that had been a time I was unhappily in love
and yet felt hopeful – hope meant now just
images and archives and a muffled street.

At last in the swirling vapour of a Bogart movie
I bought my ticket, registering I had
to change at Fornovo, and ate a warm brioche.

I was leaving Mantua. I was curiously content.
I thought of James Wright, who in a sense
I'd wronged, and of his rescue of a bee

Imprisoned in a pear beside the gasworks
outside Mantua, and of his Virgilian tag,
'the best days are the first to leave.'

As the train pulled out we entered total mist.
We choked along an isthmus, so I thought,
wholly immersed in whiteness like a veil.

'Smooth-sliding Mincius, crowned with vocal reeds,'
harsh-sliding train carrying one man
beyond all Lycidases to his Luna Park.

Last to leave! May this be my inscription!
Light and no vision, such was better than
a dream, more reassuring than oblivion.

Ahead the Apennines and knowledge that
the sun would penetrate the mist,
the soul, that passenger, stand at last

With few regrets on Platform One, changing trains,
willing to see Mantua again, hoping to make
the last days best, fleeing fast or slow.

Basta Sangue

In the National Gallery of Victoria
Is a nineteenth-century genre painting
Showing a ewe on guard beside the body
Of her dead lamb while all around her sin-
black crows stand silent in the snow. Each time
I pass the picture I find I shudder twice—
Once because good taste is now endemic
And I cannot let the sentimental go
Unsneered at—I have gone to the trouble of
Acquiring words like 'genre' and will call
Them to my aid—but secondly I know
I've been that ewe and soon will be that lamb,
That there's no way to love mankind but on
The improvised coordinates of death,
Death which rules the snow, the crows, the sheep,
The painter and the drifting connoisseur.

Enough of blood, but Abraham's raised knife
Is seldom halted and any place for God
(Even if he didn't give the orders)
Will be outside the frame. A melody
Can gong the executioner's axe awake,
A painting take away our appetite
For lunch, and mother-love still walk all night
To lull a baby quiet. Whatever gathers
Overleaf is murderous: we move
On through the gallery praising Art which keeps
The types of horror constant so that we
May go about our business and forget.

A Honeymoon in 1922

The stars will come out early, and you're tempted
To take them for those proving signs of innocence
A couple close to middle-age might need to risk
Their harmony in a hard conventicle,
And so the frisson when timidity's revoked
Starts on its pilgrimage—a short run into darkness
Or a lifelong limping past emergency.

The Old, the New, the Innocent – labels obscuring
The landscapes straight proposal of inclusion—
In Nineteen Twenty-two you take the chunking train
Up to Caboolture and then by horse and trap
On to Tewantin and its old hotel built round
A tree, and let the river whisper you to sleep
Unscorned by spotter plane, marina, surf, or sun.

Buttoned in flannelette up to the neck, the mode
Of gladiators of punt and fishing rod, racquets
Ready for a tennis afternoon, the recruits
Of urban discipline and disappointment
Move out of the sexual silence to a world
Foreshadowed by their dreams, an ancient world
Of simple movement, natural inertness.

At midnight when the bar is closed and the new moon
Shares its darkness with one sleepless phantom,
Stars having fled the scene, it might be possible
To qualify both history and geography
And rearrange the passionless disquiet

Which is Australia, placating its ancestral shapes
Whose harms and clarities bequeath such haunting nights.

Warping the sharpie to a jetty and unloading
A creel half full of whiting, flathead, bream, and one
Lone puffer-fish expiring in the bilge, with parts
Of arms reached by the sun a shade of painful salmon,
The honeymooners tell their fellow-guests they've had
A marvellous day out on the water and retire
To planetary disorder rigmaroled as love.

Both Ends Against the Middle

Deep inside the Imperial War Museum
Where children are surprised by undreamt dreams
Destruction's most impartial theorem,
The Rolls-Royce Merlin Aircraft Engine, gleams.

It seems just lowered by Donatello's tackle:
He would have known why copper pipes entwine
So murderous a tabernacle
And where control and fate might share a line.

Would we be right to look for innocence
Or guess that need to kill has shaped such grace?
Here uncompanionable Science
Is linked to everything that is the case.

In similar mode the sculptor's brilliant carving
Regains in bronze a living massacre.
Death eats, the vivid world is starving,
Each holocaust become a shepherd's star.

The Spitfire's engine's once kinetic fury
And Donatello's layered appetite
Are Humanism's judge and jury,
The Alpha and Omega of delight.

Jumping Ship

Though we shall never travel to the stars
We've put a rover on the face of Mars
And all the troubles which on earth accrue
Will soon apply to the red planet too.

The sun appears above a salmon sky
Lighting the Martian genius loci
And stalking plains, no living creature thriving,
Reveals a solemn sight, of rats arriving.

To My Granddaughters Sweeping Spelsbury Church

It's August and hay-fever weather,
We've left the house in Summer's tether—
While you girls scamper hell-for-leather
        And climb the wall
Our adult hopes are all on whether
        We'll find the Earl.

The youthful Earl of Rochester
In this small parish church interred
Proclaims the triumph of the word,
        A true contrition,
For penitence is gravely heard
        In a patrician.

A bully, fiend and alcoholic,
A brilliant Hobbesean melancholic,
A frightened sinner, parabolic,
        Yet first and foremost
A mind which rendered apostolic
        Sad Reason's ghost.

What would we find if we, instead
Of looking pious, raised the lid
Of where he lies encased in lead—
        Memento mori?
I doubt it—when the flesh has fled
        All's nugatory.

His soul which bigotry would save
Is shrunk to copper in the nave,
A mere inscription, Thus the grave
Keeps all in sight
And wife and son may only have
A year's respite.

But bouncing through the door, you girls
Pounce on the verger and with skirls
Of laughter, sudden whirls and curls,
Take up his broom,
Then, like George Herbert, for the Earl's
Sake sweep the room.

When Martha and Amelia raise
A little dust to rightly praise
The magnitude of other days,
They're only playing—
It's Grandad's pompous paraphrase
Which is dismaying.

Life works the other way around:
It's what George Herbert saw which wound
His metaphor into his sound—
A parish priest,
He'd keep his ear to the ground
This much at least.

So give the verger back his broom
And let the Earl sleep out his doom,
I must return to London soon
    And you to Rome—
Though you're not Catholic, you assume
    There, God's at home.

Is Oxfordshire more savoury
Than the ill-swept Trastavere?
Is Rome all foreign knavery?
    Our cows are mad,
Our people sunk in slavery,
    Our climate bad.

But still we speak a language which
The whole world seems to have an itch
To learn, and this may make you rich—
    England supporters—
And since you don't stray on the pitch,
    Dutiful daughters.

MAX IS MISSING

Streetside Poppies

After fifty years of writing poetry
I lust still for what is natural.

My vernacular was always bookish;
somehow I missed the right Americans,

I couldn't meld the High and Low –
even my jokes aspired to footnotes –

but I am open to Wordsworthian signs.
Along the Via Flaminia the whole

of Rome's rebuilding, cobbles
like liquorice blocks in Piazza del Popolo

and flowering by a building site
'a thin red line' of city poppies.

Time to abort my years of affectation:
burn, you petals, confront Bernini,

remember the queue of conquerors
from Alaric to General Clark.

History has clogged the open city
of the heart: it's sixty feet above

its early certainties and I
can visit churches only for the Art.

The rain's been heavy and the scarlet
of the poppies is flambeau'd along

the verge's dark viridian.
Nature, with Roman gravitas,

draws eyes away from angel angles
down to a footsore gallantry of blooms.

Max is Missing

The stars are there as mathematics is,
The very there of nothing to be proved.

And so we say that theorems rely
On axioms or proof by the absurd.

The stars outshine the tenses, kings on plinths,
And each enigma of the numerate,

While all along our mathematicians fear
They're stalking-horses of an abstract god,

And posit the suspicion there's no room
For rich historic tit-bits in their space –

The big and little of it, shrunk or spun,
A million needle-points, a 'Mono-Ange'.

Out of the corner of Philosophy's eye
A Mathematician's pinning on a post

Max is missing: ginger tabby cat
With white sabots – reward for his return.

The government of integers will wait
While our researcher searches for his cat,

The stars be patient, God donate his time –
A theorem is for Christmas, but a cat

Is for forever. Come home, Maximus,
The magnets on the fridge are slipping down.

The page is Luddite quite as stars are bright,
A ball-point and a brain out-twinkle them.

Should stars know Max is missing, would they guess
How little he must miss them where he is?

A Butterfly Stampede

Softest of God's creatures ganging up
on a loner, toiling stoic
terraces of olive trees –
                                        can they be Furies
these companionable shutters?

Could they brave shades of time, so little
and so desperate? Or quiver through the air
in serious rhapsody?
                                        In history will souls
recall these flimsiest of comrades?

Swarming butterflies at altitudes
above the wasps, serving in an airy tongue
the primal plebiscite:
                                        quick go words which match
the needs of mannequins and mites.

In theory these could be that whelming
catalepse of one foot stamping some
disaster's timbre –
                                        be calm, O urban mind,
such are just farfalle mustering.

A ghost of city man, he cared today
to save a spider from a shiny bath –
so let him cool himself
                                        with fans of butterflies
and pick a grape for Tantalus.

O Nature! O Conspiring Mind! O Capitalising
Poetry! Rise on the thermals of a swarm
of butterflies.
                                        Hadrian's little soul has multiplied
to blot out death as soon as laughter.

The Last Hours of Cassiodorus

God is laying his last slate to the roof,
The ceiling of my death is near complete,
The Vivarium must now live up to its name.

Fish in my stewponds circle silently;
Their free captivity is like the soul,
An endless round, then thrashing in a net.

Our state days pinioned in official letters,
The *Variae* of sound administration,
But Boethian birds still shun my volary.

Home to the South, to sad Scolacium
From Civilisation and a Library,
The sea spray drying on acacia leaves.

After me, what further barbarisms?
My pose is prayer but yet my head is filled
With the terrifying dissonances of God.

I have lived well past my statutory days;
The mapping pen has fallen from my hands,
A hundred years or more of beating wings.

So Unimaginably Different and So Long Ago

We who would probably want to remake
or at least tidy up Tracey Emin's bed
and mostly expect to find our pill-dispensers
in some pharmaceutical cupboard other
than Damien Hirst's, or prefer a child's
kaleidoscope showing a rose-windowed
sunburst to a Gilbert and George blood-test –
we, the uncomfortable in our century,
are equally discomfited by this
display of five-hundred-years-dead craftsmen's
masterpieces blooming in six rooms.

We stare amazedly at a Saint Sebastian
by Pete the Poulterer, are bewitched by
a bust of a Medici by Handy Andy
aka 'Hawkeye goes to Florence',
judge if The Filipino Kid or Street-Cred Larry
carries off the prize among Madonnas
doused in blue and dazzle. What is it here
which harries us? We don't believe in progress
yet how can taste run backwards? We walk home knowing,
whichever of its great ones measures it,
the world must fall a God's length short of God.

Streamers

To get away, to make your fortune, to lose your virginity,
you hold one end of a coloured streamer
as R.M.S. *Otranto* snaps the paper symmetry
of country, identity and all your loved ephemera.

And if you remember the ribbon roads with their ribbon
    banners
out from a capital city, flaring on the used car lots,
you swap them for Literature and kinsman Arcite's hots
for Emily, advancing his 'streamer', Mars to Diana.

Then the creeks once known to you as spider defences
on the school's Cross Country Run, become the babble
of a Tuscan stream, *torrente* to Serchio's dry tenses.

Now see where something or other streams in the firmament.
Christ's blood, human destiny, language's gabble?
A straight line is not the shortest distance between two
    points.

Tasso's Oak

Down from the cloistered calm of San Onofrio
Tasso came to lean against his tree,
All Rome before his gaze and every bridge
And house and market filled with dirt, and palaces
The filthiest things of all. The news was better –
Not many days from now he'd been assured
Great Rome itself would crown him laureate,
His madness turn divine and all the madmen
In the world's insanitary pit
Rejoice that of their number, one was recognised.
But where in final vindication would
Innocence survive, some true thing ringed
By nature as this oak was in its bole?
And where was honesty not reliant on
The shifts of fortune? The oak was young or not
As old as he, and stood for what he'd been
When his intelligence was pure ambition,
When nature had a skin which welcomed pain
As soon as ecstasy. The world was business
And the poet an emphatic businessman –
This was the health of things, but everywhere
His gift reminded him that jewellery shone
Like sickness, that blood dried on the fingernails
Of rulers, belvedered with whisperings
In roses or locked where light would never pass.
The fault was Poetry's, those words which clashed
Like blades but never joined the field, the sound
Of truth but bearing no true weight, the brain

Unable to baptise the conquered heart.
It was the poet's calligram to match
Power with imagination, chart time's
Collision with the tongue, and choose among
The many madnesses, state melancholy.
If the mind's locked up for longer than the body,
Attrition's tedium may bring life down
From sacred heights to watch the valley floor
Where men and women do not bother with
The light forever changing in the clouds.
This was his Rome and this was how the oak
Would buttress him, its newness in his arms.

The Philosophers' Garden

If on your way to The Tomb where today
they are demonstrating how the stone was rolled away
you cross our small North London Park
and by avoiding the roller-blading children
you take a slightly longer route, you'll find
yourself skirting 'The Philosophers' Garden',
a small crepuscular fenced-off area
announcing itself proudly by so grand
a name. No dogs may enter and no children,
thereby blocking off a half of what
philosophers disdain. Tree cover is intensely green
verging on the black; flowering shrubs have left
to join the noisy world and dampness promises
a Schopenhauerian grave-light through the day.
Unlike the voices hovering here, the place
is modest rather as a Corot sighted in
a provincial gallery, and the smell
of dogshit drifts within its purlieus. 'Dog', says
someone in the Peripateia, 'a glance
back at the spirit world', and as for 'shit'
that's what they call 'detritus' if they have
to speak their native tongue. We settle down
on most uncomfortable benches while
the cursive learning we are forced to hear
drones on, so proud of its great outwardness.
From these dark lines the People's Park seems odd
and hardly plangent, with its bouncing balls,
its ice-cream haloes and injunctions to
the fainter civic courtesies. But here

the rotund ones may read the wind: they note
on Ariel's Web a spidery message – *The Rich*
can't die! Dishevelled lie in swathes the souls
of the imponderent, and *Russell's Tiger*
is behind that shelf of bellarmines.
The colder parts of sun are honoured for
their cleaner light and nothing will earn points
unless its jargon is free-standing. Poets
say they think that song is best *Moll Dur*,
but for philosophy the fastened gates
of any Major are the only truth.
Don't speak here of mutability,
or suggest that you learned evil at your family's
breast, at school or at a job – they'll paint
you in an older garden, one outgrown
by this luxurious seclusion, weaned from
the knowledgeable by Eden's balmy weather.
So now you know – it was worth the trouble
to unlock the stiff and halting gate and find
a hosed-down seat; philosophy is what
made sense at the Expulsion: it was a grid
to hang on when the nerves were sheared away.
It sat along with politics to replan Nature –
witness the leaves like helicopter blades,
the sure eclipse of sun. We feel our clothes
for dampness, start to hear the sounds our seriousness
had banished – surely those are buses straining
up the hill; that seismic shift's from trainers

in their thousands after school. Tiptoe
through the gate, rejoin the unaccountable:
our positive despair will always keep
our prisoned bodies fearful of fences.

Magica Sympathia

Lord Herbert of Cherbury
Lounges in a thicket
Like an unpicked strawberry,
Isaac Oliver, pinxit.

Montgomery Parish Church
Keeps all the little Herberts
As terracotta dolls. Which
One is George the Wordsmith?

Magic fills the landscape –
What, here in Wales?
A flowery English handshake
For Llandrindod Wells?

Windfarm propellers' traction
Turns a Lute Book's pages,
Victorian reticulation
Laps Vyrnwy's emerald edges.

Ask the hawks which hover
Over Dinas Vawr's sheep
Who if not Glendower
Talks rivers up from creeks?

Those plush hermetic demons
Who internationalise
Wye and Lugg and Severn
Are worth a Latin phrase.

The Past is why the Present
Is packed for the Co-op.
It is and yet it isn't
That time must have a stop.

O Sympathetic Magic,
Shy fortresses and weirs!
O Forests Green and Stygic,
The wit of Passing Stairs!

Lord Herbert gave his castle
Up to Cromwell's men,
He held himself a vassal
Only to song and pen.

Hermetically Sealed or What the Shutter Saw

(A photograph of 1911)

The stifling air of Brisbane, cleansed by time,
Shows the family *Main* Easter-Islanded in sepia,
Slow shutters making them North British as indeed
They were, though stiffly suited as befits Colonials
Steeled for success. Through this the mercantile's
Made magical; it puts a fearful competence
In frame – Behold a portrait truly *feierlich*
And God-like, humanity a Middle Class *ex voto*.

Pater Familias, mustachio'd, dewlapped, forty-four
But seeming sixty, the God Mark Main turns everything
He looks at into Glasgow – surrounded by his family,
His liver undercutting his immortal soul,
He practises Theocracy. He is informing us
That through the doors which whisky opens, soon or late,
Comes Death the Factor, a well-born trader and therefore
Your family must be properly dressed to welcome him.

His stern and English wife, Mae Simms, uncloned
In whitest lace, a Beatrice of new-built Randwick,
Overlooks the paddock of her hopes. She has the discipline
Of Start Again, a cure for each indisposition:
Fate washes us to peccant shores, but we must keep
The absolute commandments – sons and daughters are
what's left of angels in a fallen universe.
The sun shines through us yet we are the North.

Enthroned in pole position on the left,
Their eldest child, their daughter Marion, sets her face
Into a tuneless cameo: dark-skinned and Pictish,

She gives posterity and photographer no hint
She is an anarch of dejection, a humorist
Of hopelessness. Her bust is tightly fronted, balcony
Of soft dictatorship. She is to be my Mother and will stay
Younger than I forever, her hand enclosing mine.

Behind the seated seniors, two sons, Eric and Neville,
Endorse expectancy and youth, the ichor of their promise
Destined never to dry. Waistcoats, watches fobbing off
The larrikin enticement of their sex, they're blessed
With god-like blindness – they will never see their graves
In France. Perhaps none in the group would know them
On death's wharf. 'Magnificently unprepared', a poet said,
But seldom life's long littleness like this.

Dolly and Winnie, indomitable and plastic sisters –
Dolly a headscarfed *Carmen* extra, Winnie the beauty
With a gaze as basilisk as Passover.
Harder than teenage light, their understanding
Of our fallen natures keeps them well abreast of
War, Depression, Real Estate, Survival –
We have to die, they say, but seaside houses
And golf courses shall be our proper recompense.

Little Roy, who will disgrace them all and as
My Uncle Mick will be a Tattersalls Club bookie
After meningitis makes his Proteus, is just in front
Of Edna, baby of the family, a sweet, buck-toothed
Forensic angel – strange that the chief executive
Of God in this our Family Tenebrae should be

The youngest. From birth she'll know how best
To fend off pain with laughter, work and kindliness.

With seven children who will produce only six
Grandchildren, the parental psychopomps beckon to
Their descendant, a paltry straggler of the age
They were so proud to own. Time's not an integer
Of true forgiveness, but perhaps they wish
The world were spiked with magic, and that their
Materialistic gods might hatch on blankness to become
The fattest schoolboy silkworms of their hopes.

Deo Gratias Anglia

England where the natives speak in iambic pentameter.
Preston Merchant

So when the moon is high an ancient spell
Falls on the sons of Milton, Donne and Pope
And Londoners converse in perfect numbers.
Dismantled orthodoxy goes on dreaming,
Its baffled children feeling on their faces
One light and then one heavy drop of rain.

Calumny

The writer who has turned remorse to habit
keeps coming back to his decreed disaster,
his métier, as God's devised by Heine,
the lure of forgiveness and its *alter*,
self-denunciation; and so foreground
is cleared among the mental junk, designer-
allegory, language lesions, doubtful
analogues of Science; his practice like the
widowed Queen's, to be an *underliner*.

In unsophisticated youth he'd settle
at his desk and feel his fangs obtruding
on his lower lip, his copra'd hair appear
along his back of hands, the poison clicking
in his keys, the untrue and the vicious
chastened by his insight – not a career
but yet a veiled vocation, this unswerving
challenge to the everyday by a no one
out of nowhere, fearful and austere.

It was quite otherwise, the world continued
unreformed and his objective satire
forced him to take himself as subject-matter –
Applausus! It surprised him that another
whom he mourned should be a source of favour.
But words like seeds or bullets merely scatter
emotions to the wind and human feelings
follow tracks so general the public
hears its own heart-rending in the clatter.

Spurious erudition goes on winging
its way into his frozen heart, asserting
he is too respectable to die; a
kingdom peaceable as love is waiting
just for him, extinction countermanded.
He can't believe it, always his desire
is for the species to be fenced with calumny
and she he loved there, doing without justice,
her face lit still by self-deploring fire.

The Man Who Knew Everybody

Inside his racquet cover
a note from Misia Sert
and the faintly yellow hankie
used to wipe sweat off at the Finals
in Bordeaux – he's rushing home to change
to meet that Englishman who runs
New Verse and who is bringing him a message
from the uncircumcised Auden.

The decades change so swiftly
this might be the Via Botteghe Oscure
with Roman urchins thick as partridges
about his legs, and the marvellous boy
encountered yesterday beside a fountain
talking to the pigeons. 'I've called this one
Connolly, he's cornered all the crumbs,
and where the hell is Ostia? I'm supposed
to declaim there by the prick-proud sea.'

While convoys shuddered through
the Atlantic night, his own war effort
was re-reading the established classics –
could all this death be the proper price to pay
so Stendhal might feel sorry for himself
and Flaubert hone his prose?

Like him those guys weren't queer.
Hard that – heterosexuality in a century
such as this. It'll come back, said the Big Man
in the Villa. Uranian Love is envy,
a sort of Roman twist to Hellenism,
so very gladiatorial.

What sadness to have lost
American simplicity and innocence,
the Jamesian profile of an honest soul
amid the European shadows. Here
people will perform textbook obscenities
for a chocolate bar or twenty cigarettes,
and these catarrhal frogs are cousins to the ones
which croaked for Hannibal.

The old philosopher
is partying tonight – 'Dear Boy,
you find me very busy. I'm rehearsing
for this evening – if I put Peggy "there",
she'll be the Speaker of the House
and call them to her one by one.'

Whatever happens next
there'll be a name to hail, even as far
as twilight homes in Michigan
with floodlit tennis courts. The Thirties,
Forties, Fifties – how many decades still to come?

The evening has grown visionary,
assignations keep on piling up
and haloed in the Southern light there stands
another gawky prodigy to get to know.

Ex Libris Senator Pococurante

Carchemish, this tedious performance
our forefathers valued as the first account
of the creation of the world; it seems
no more than a boring battle between
the snakes and the dogs, with comic referees
called gods obsessed by their own dignity.

The Troiliad, just as silly and twice as long,
with lists of heroes, ships and towns,
interfering gods on shortest fuses
and magic implements and animals,
its love-life platitudinous
and its epithets attached like luggage labels.

The Hunnish Wars, a propaganda feast
prepared by an ambitious consul
for home advantage, as full of lies
as tedium. The style is gelid,
the facts fictitious – it deserves its fate
to end up teaching grammar to dull boys.

Summa Cattolica, a sort of Natural History
of Credulity. Should you want to know
the stories of the saints you still might baulk
at being shown their laundry lists and tax returns.
This huge concordance mixes pedantry
with gloating martyrdom and police reports.

The Satanic Comedy, a strange attempt
to draw a picture of the world based on
the machinations of a city council
together with a paedophile's infatuation
with a merchant's teenage daughter.
In three books, Heaven, Hell and Nowhere.

Eden's End. Expelled from Heaven in a war
with guns and bombs, The Devil tempts
God's franchise-takers with his fruits and hisses.
Our classicist author makes Adam a market
gardener while Eve assembles Lifestyle hints
on Post-Coital Guilt and PMT.

The Interlude. In this almost unending
meditation on the life and times of one
banal existence, the author dares presume
we are as self-obsessed as he is.
Its marginal attractions are no better:
country hovels, childhood and wet walks.

Donovan's Demise, the lexicon of Modernism,
its every sentence stitched into the text
like Cash's name-tapes, this epyllion
of solipsism demands that we devote
a lifetime to its study. Properly examined
it becomes the scribblings on a ouija-board.

AFTERBURNER

Deuterothanatos

I have found a poem in your childish hand
carefully dated, 'aged thirteen years, ten months',
which speaks of 'the low golden light'
and of the coming of what, unknown to you
as such, is surely death. Though we are born
once only, we die several times. If our
single entitled death defines us, something
of it may be shown beforehand. In
the poem you greet the unknown greater world
with a sweet bold welcoming sign, almost
an entreaty. But what confidence remains
that on that lonely morning when you died
your seeming change proved true, and that those calm
confiding words had not been overwhelmed
by terror? I see myself revealed
in solemn Greek proceeding hand-in-hand
with airborne Hermes, second-
guessing what's to come – with you ahead,
the light already low, and perhaps goldening.

The Rider Haggard Window, St Mary's, Ditchingham

Time which eats the stories of our lives
Preserves a cruel freshness here to show
How energetic certainty contrives
To tell us what we think we almost know:
The warlike God of England will bestow
At least in retrospect on loyal wives
A school apotheosis, dirge of knives,
With dying, quick in life, in glass made slow.

A dubious transfer this, as history cools,
An ancient trespass, but a change of rules.
The world was opening which today is closed,
And where the mind went, destiny would tread
With God and Science noisily opposed
And story-telling garlanding the dead.

The Man Who Spoke in Tongues

He found he couldn't find his hand
once here today was gone demain.

His train ran fast, his train ran slow,
but he got off at Subito.

Those Pentecostal flowers he bloomed
were multi-cultured in one room.

His watch sat silent on the table –
time was another Eurofable.

On isles where parts of speech were pigs
he truffled up some infra digs.

Having to leave the colloquy
he made his anthropology.

His every course had as its par
the contents of the minibar.

When Lawrence-like they buggered him,
he cried aloud in acronym.

And knew, with no word of a lie,
a thousand ways to say Goodbye.

Sex and the Over-Seventies

You thought it wouldn't worry you again
but comes this Second Adolescence,
the never-mastered stripping of the Bren.

And now the bodies cease to rhyme –
disappointments not relieved by joking,
dignity grown hirsute by the hour.

The curse of Literature – MacNeice's Horace's
Lycidas, who makes young men a furnace,
is only a midnight memory of Boarding School.

Hope to be someone's 'Ancient Person of My Heart'
or even a 'Maimed Debauchee' –
better than Herr Aschenbach on beach patrol.

And cringe when fellow-males anatomize
delusions of their female friends
with vernal blood-flow from sarcoma sacs.

It's late and you and your body
are alone – keep talking, to delay
having to go upstairs together.

Horace's Odes Translated

The fine scribes of America are herded here together,
The subsidized Aediles, the Ivy League Grammarians,
  compilers of historically flattering parallels,
  beneficiaries of a Military-Industrial Estate –

all are between the covers of a well-printed book
to honour the lightly louche Italic poet who
  loved both boys and girls and knew best how to please
  the hard men of his time while nudging memories

of Nature on remote selections and showing how
Republican directness could mutate to slaves' long service
  (a dab hand at rebuking lusts of gilded youth
  while hinting at the use a girl might put her bangles to),

but always and ever the querulous protester at
fate and extinction, whether wandering after Philippi
  or narrowly missed by an old and rotten tree,
  reborn among the countrymen of Bly and Cage.

Throughout this book the Classically-conscious reader
can scarcely avoid the shadow of a new Imperium
  falling on the old: after all, the Parthians inhabited
  what is now Iraq, and it upset the Emperor

when one of his pet legions was brought home
in body bags – nor do the parallels stop there
  since the English Augustans still haunt the stacks
  and every university seeks a personal Maecenas.

Was it all so unimaginably different and all so long ago?
What stays the same is place-making, pleasing the Sub-Dean,
   keeping language Pastoral while hinting sex and booze
   may, after all, be just another way of working out.

Eheu fugaces – we learn to sigh and greet a Postumus
in every generation with comradely decorum –
   America may pass away, and Europe, but will singers
   of tomorrow's *carmina* reflect their world so well?

Rimbaud's Ostrich

He didn't need one, he was an animal,
The animal which outmanoeuvred Europe.
But in the photograph, as on a boot-polish lid,
The ostrich struts cross-legged, a mapping stool.
Harar is four thousand miles from Paris.
And just a Metro ride from two World Wars.

We should ask the ostrich what it thinks
Of scholarship, or lurid nights with absinthe,
Of being in the months of love for essay prizes,
The coal-smoke-crystalled walls of Camden Town,
The semi-educated painters jetting in
To put some Prester John in Cork Street daubs.

France deserved this tribal fetishism,
Its language had become mere logarithm,
Its classicism a blunt guillotine.
Supposing Rimbaud met Sir Richard Burton,
They would have ridden ostriches round town
To startle the solared anthropologists.

Afterburner

For John Tranter

I knew I wasn't saying anything like exactly
what I meant, but I knew as well that it was what
I had to say. All art, I proceeded with, springs
from exaggeration, and this is due to linear time's
sheer wastefulness as a tool of understanding.

I went to the theatre, despite being warned by those
who know its dangers, and heard such 'mighty lines'
as would never be allowed in Court. Truth
to life, the programme claimed, is not the only end,
the rules insist that lives be syntax-swathed.

My neighbour had upset a tense soliloquy by opening
a box of chocolates and I noticed two young men
touching each other in the row in front. I lost the words
but gained instead a quizzical smell of almonds
and the envious quiver of remembered sex.

Yet this was strange: after some hundred hours of theatre-
going, thousands of days equipped with books and discs,
I was being tipped backwards into the sawdust memories
of down-the-road, trying to set a sort of Scrapbook up –
my childhood, such a provincial world to be born into.

Still, I knew my real concern was 'What is fuel
for understanding?' Wordsworth had to be born somewhere
and so did Wittgenstein. Back to exaggeration –
the after-shave sophistication of an uncle
was Murdoch, Mozart and Malvolio, depending.

It was then I set out on a trek for metaphor –
the missing M was money, but alas I wasn't good
at that – I got it mixed with envy, itself of course
a perfectly proper subject for research – I'd taken
eleven shillings back to school as pocket money.

A temporary assurance and dismallest companion.
Hope was running out and in a Time of Tangents
I couldn't go full-frontal. I'd open the box and so
release some old retired irrelevances, especially
The Thirty-Nine Articles of Flower Arranging.

I'd been raised an Anglican. 'In the Name of the Larder,
the Bun and the Mouldy Toast.' 'We have left undone
those things which we ought to have done.' The choir entered
with Brasso'd Cross, and the Greek Girl's breasts were
antiphoning in her sweater. I knew I loved music more than people.

The trouble was I was ten and forty and seventy and . . .
what was I? Seriously devoid of tenses for a start.
Where Jacobean poets used to fill their poems
with the very latest scientific instances, I reached
for a handbook and straightway witnessed 'Afterburn'.

So this was the glow at the tail end of my life,
this was the exaggeration I'd served so long,
the boosters were behind and what burned now
was all the fuel of living left – ahead
the prelinguistic purlieus of the gods.

The Last Wave Before the Breakwater

The engine dies. The dream has by degree
Come to where the green is lightening, the rocks
Are somewhere in the civil distance – sea
Is moving up in mist, a paradox
Within this calm. Something is now to be.

The storm is distant, just the lights behind
The eyes are left of lightning's ambuscade,
But still the swell is present in the mind
And now the panoply of waves is made
By memory and allegory combined.

And it is here, the last surviving wave
Which starting years away was following,
A true occasion which the heart might save
Its courage for. A very little thing,
It says to die, to rhyme into a grave.

And know the dreaming self will not relent
Or convalescent mind afford its hope,
The voyage ending here before its end,
No harbour lights, no casting of a rope,
Wordless, auxiliary and irredent.

In a Time of the Wilting of Poinsettias

That Christmas is a secular feast
Few could deny or likely wish
Were otherwise, and so at least
    It will be thought outlandish

That presents round the plumpish tree
Swelling the profits of the Bourse
And profaning the Nativity
    Should seem par-for-the-course

Of ignorant consumerism –
Go draw a better gentler line,
Say through a giving gesture's prism
    The light of love might shine –

See stacked up on the carpet's pile
Appropriate or unwanted things
(*You're worth it, you're an audiophile*)
    As Christmas Morning brings

New Magi to suburban lords,
With carols from King's College or
Bach's camels at the Jordan's fords,
    Sit-Coms and Shows galore

To mark the presence of a God
Not gone away, just lower wattage,
The Casa Santa where He trod
    Transported to Swiss Cottage.

And now the strangest gifts are strewn
Beside the electronic Crib
Unseasonal poinsettias soon
Gone like Sennacherib

In briefest scarlet metaphor,
Poor tropic-loving petals forced
To feign eternal Summer for
A cold doctrinal North.

But theirs will be an apogee
Indifferent to the handset's search,
Not showering leaves round the TV
But properly in church.

Look almost anywhere in Rome:
Ablaze in ranks of white and red,
Poinsettias blooming far from home!
Christ's living spirit fled

From Time to Cross and Altar and
Ciborium – the white His semen,
The red the suture of His hand,
Duality His demon.

A mobile in a tourist's coat
Reorders the Canonic Hours.
Inexorably downward float
The spent incarnate flowers.

Stravinsky in Hollywood

You couldn't call it exile – after all
Just down the road we have a Venice,
A resting place to keep Diaghilev warm,
And all the Session Men are bronzed from tennis:
Europe's a library away, a pall
Of something chemical hangs over us.
I told them, 'Sunless as a mushroom farm.'

'Shall we listen to my Mass before
We get drunk?' Home we know is in the head,
And up the road somewhere the Schönberg train
Is crossing points into the Classic Shed –
Not the Neo-Classic! A Priceless Law!
God is good: work tells us what is God.
In California Abel murders Cain.

Shorty Rogers on the flugelhorn,
I can make something great from that.
Divide my years by Mozart's – goes three times
Almost. Everyone here's some sort of Expat,
Just like Adam. I dreamt that money was a lawn,
I mowed it, stuffed it in my agent's hat.
The studios are filming Europe's crimes.

You praise God with some skill if you have any,
But all sounds must be heard and not just written.
No paper music, no new Adorno rules,
No Kleenex tears, like Mr Britten's –
Here's Herman, Woody; Goodman, Benny,

Indexed with Huxley's *Doors* and Walter's baton,
A change of steersman on *The Ship of Fools*.

I put the carnal bells of marriage in
My compositions once and now they sound
The tocsin of my end – perhaps not yet!
Since memory may grow on any ground,
To eat the past is spirit's discipline
And Ariel's new words must be designed
Among the broken letters of the alphabet.

BETTER THAN GOD

Better Than God

As He said of the orchestra
at the Creation, *they can play*
anything you put in front of them.

The Apprentice's Sorcerer

In Geneva in a plague-deep hole,
Recreating how the universe began,
In heat as keen as God's impulsive plan,
Scientists seek to animate the soul
Of everything that's classified as Life,
Victor Frankenstein's convulsions, Cain's Stanley knife.

Somewhere a little knowledge starts to gesture.
It may be dangerous but it's enterprise;
It levels difference in weight and size;
Its beauty is of skin and not in vesture –
This is the secret of the lead made gold,
The bread from stone, a timeless Paradise on hold.

The world looks on: so Paracelsian
Such hubris and such cost! What is there still
To do to prove Creation's codicil?
And is this Back to Basics or Caesarian
To keep your figure, as the Magi squat
Around the Electronic Crib at Santa's Weinacht Grot.

Apprentices galore have heard the call –
Ives' and Stevens's Insurance days,
Pascal's mathematics second-guessed as praise,
Hopkins' Ignatian Exercises stalled.
Many have shunned the rules to get to grips
With a broadband innovation of Apocalypse.

Empowered by forces somehow empathised,
A personal or general Crusade
May go awry: the pendant legal blade
Reflecting love of Reason and its prized
And ironising power may fall on throats
Which called for Joachim's Heaven or Universal Votes.

Each innovator served an inner voice
Superbly iterating sounds of Truth,
Some from a lifetime's wisdom, some from youth,
And none believing they had any choice –
But who among these bristling handers-down
Of the Aurora of New Birth knew verb from proper noun.

Perhaps in this Swiss Hole the world will see
A proof beyond its statutory Big Bang
And hear that what the Morning Angels sang
Was more than some wide-screened banality.
The love which moves the sun and the other stars
Is syntax-negligent, and may never parse.

We do Not Write the Way We Are

My Mother was more a Small Investor
than she was Queen Clytemnestra
but she bought me shares in dreams,
in doing not what is, but seems –
you start out rhyming, she declared,
but go your own way into dread
        with bed sores and bad words.

Orestes' and Electra's Mum
was, in their view, the Higher Scum.
I loved my Mother and I tried
to feel less guilty, so I cried,
but in those dreams she willed me have
I dug around her missing grave –
        now write that up, she said.

I do not write the way I am,
I rode on a storm when I sat in a tram,
my fears were highly rational
but only when I dreamed – The Fall
was daily life, the Workers' Wheel,
the tangled web we're told we weave,
        the millions historied.

How do we scan the things we write?
Is this our fabled Second Sight,
the huge reflective Self interred
in generations of the Word?
I'd love to pose as Terrorist

or Trotsky under House Arrest,
        but sadly I'm not mad.

Instead, a circumstantial Truth
without the vanity of proof
is mixing in my double mind
with darkness lining up behind,
an unfree kind of Free Trade Zone,
a Fascist rule insisting words
        report to me alone.

Whereof We Cannot Speak

There is nothing here 'whereof'. We are
philosophers and drainmakers,
prospectus-holders, vainly gripping
the under-edge of a minor star.

On which we know we can't stay quiet.
How many sonnets must we write
before the great gong sounds in Heaven?
And is this calm a call to riot?

A species which feels sorry for
not just itself, but worms and bats,
would like to make life fair and take
the wrinkles out of sex and war.

Under the microscope it seems
to be covered in odd parasites
called words, and like the pigeon must
talk to walk, nodding at dreams.

Self-lecturing, it fills the Hall
with topoi and parameters
and delegates with names on badges
fulminating where they sprawl.

The brain floats on a lake of words,
just as once the world was held
on elephant-back above a sea –
subversive rhyme suggests that herds

Of metaphors with sharper beak
tear at the silence of unease:
a philosopher feels on his cheek
the tears whereof he cannot speak.

That War is the Destruction of Restaurants

All occasions bloom within priorities.
Insensible and more insensible selves
Choose to marry in their most-frayed cuffs.

They are promising riches in the Afterlife
Where every thread unravelling is a star
Within a plain of anecdotal stars.

This is the only true intelligence
Of taste: you open eyes in infancy
And see a dog in death-throes from a bait.

The prunus clipped, a glorious parent and
A fearful one speak of themselves at tea.
The five-foot line is waiting to usurp.

Like God, our animators are upset
By nought on nought, always too many noughts –
Stop dying now, they say to Dacca floods.

In Pantheons the heroes may not snore
Or be androgynous in twilight tombs
Since sexual peace is firmly cut in stone.

Year on year the wars arrive and raze
The science plains: we want to order fire
And do so staring at the plat-du-jour.

A Very Forgiving Medium

Our landlord's man has let us off this time,
        We're not expelled.
Victorians liked their mortar made with lime,
        Our walls have held.

A very forgiving medium, it seems,
        Not like cement
Which struts and strangles until roofs and beams
        Are racked and rent.

Round here the jerry-built and stucco'd blocks
        From Hardy's Age
Have huge exciting windows, paradox
        Of bird and cage

Whose first proprietors sang by coal-fires
        The servants set,
Whose morals were adjacent their desires
        To have and get.

Their cold-faced world turned them to optimists;
    However hard
To be In Trade and climb the Social Lists,
        The Visiting Card

Was trusted to revoke Equality,
        That careless turn
Which might mean daughters' tears, a son at sea,
        The ash-filled urn.

Their slapdash heirs, rent-paying Arrivistes
    From anywhere,
Prefer a nervous vigil to a feast,
    And stair by stair

Mount to a tower where their metered gaze
    Tracks modern living,
A limeless medium, fallen on hard days
    And unforgiving.

Leafing Through the Latin Dictionary

Fuga, fugas – music now, not back
at school where Harry Roberts flashed his gown,
a toga to berate a class as slack
as Rome became; we'd been meant to be
English Augustans, but were soon brought down
to being worthy only of a few
emotive Saxon nouns and verbs: the sea
had brought our fathers to a sanded shore,
packed tight with iron sermons on The Poor –
but still the dictionary had work to do:
peregrinus, wanderers in need
of some Virgilian outcome – might this book
have shown how Europe's words could safely bleed
on strands Aeneas left to Captain Cook?

Oppidanus – not from Rome, but not
from Eton either; if from anywhere
we hailed from pissed-on concrete and caked snot,
a gravel-rash battalion called up for
training in Real Estate and prostate snips –
no worse for that, but somewhere off there lurked
a world whose words were from a greater law,
the Pax Britannica, a king in sight,
an Empire wider than a day and night,
the home boys set to die among the ships –
spero, spes – we hoped, and now it's here,
the Trading-Up Republic, confident
of its own sparky Roman atmosphere
and *timeo*, to fear the gifts we're sent.

Voltaire's Allotment

All Paris is a banlieu, as all
Cities everywhere are vile
As written to by St Paul.

Therefore what I choose to cultivate,
Like an attendant servant's smile,
Is the allotment of debate.

Those small sections tucked behind
Pantheons and the Monarch's Mile
Are death warrants yet unsigned.

They are not properly gardens,
Have no reticulating tile
Or Le Nôtre's marching margins.

Meanwhile, in the theatre and in pages
Of classically clanking style
I circulate for fame and wages.

What I sow is European opinion,
Shallots to tingle and beguile,
Not the full apocalyptic onion.

Sitting at a liberal ruler's board,
Talking hangman's talk the while,
I strip notes from the common chord.

Finally, for my bequest, I leave
A new church, 'a sumptuous pile',
And, duly on Revolution's eve,

As reliquary of Rousseau,
The tears of Europe in a phial
And the allotments where they grow.

In Bed with Oblomov

I know you'd rather sleep alone,
Ilya Ilyich, but you are safe with me,
As I am Sleep myself, your own
Entitlement to common harmony
And I can promise you no dream
Will trouble you – like pretty women who
Are also nice, or friends who seem
True friends, yet truly too good to be true,
Or servant faithful in her heart,
A cook as simple and as scrupulous
As porridge, or the teasing art
Of *Casta diva*, or the endless fuss
Of paying visits before noon
Or obligations running with the clock –
Let these be banished like the moon,
You are with me; that bang was not a knock!
Beyond your windows Russia sleeps
In snow, as drifts, which may not even be,
Surround your resting; vacant deeps
Soul-white but bled into the wintersea,
So many ice-bound paper ports
Which Czars have deemed our Western Doors
While civil servants class the sorts
Of overdue reforms we stall by wars.
Give up the world, even when awake,
Attain a glorious discontinuancy
Where sunlight is a guilty fake –
Let someone clean the room, but be with me

At drowsing's edge and share the dust
Which lullabies the noise of coach and street.
Pull blankets up, give it your trust,
This love-bed made for just one pair of feet.

Henry James and Constipation

The mail creeps into Florence with the sun
And I, along these lotus-lettered tiles,
Touch at the door of Disappointment; smiles
Of fellow-guests I am ashamed to shun
Adorn the corridors and I assume
The living William's in a letter in my room.

Your strictures, William, if I call them thus,
Are Medical Injunctions, similar
To that one body-mind self-avatar
We hold is Moral Truth. The impetus
Of our distinct decorums, like our bowels,
Stays with the Signoria and the men with trowels.

Why do we quit our shores of sense to seek
Something no better, but much longer known?
Their mason's trowels! We think, perhaps we've sown
The present with the past. Is Boston weak
In wanting to declare a glorious pose
Just truths a waiter winks or scholar might disclose?

Dear Henry, says the word-within-the-words,
You've eaten Europe, now digest it well:
Alice, yourself, all Jameses should dispel
Inheritance, as migratory birds,
Wingspanned enough, approach the classic coasts
Of Excellent Ambush, hangman's shadows, faction's ghosts.

The pills are packed, small dictionaries of hope,
Encyclopaedias encroaching on
The atlas where the motorist may swan
The shore. Old Europe's by new Huxleyan soap
Made clean. One half-Swiss hint from Burckhardt and
All art lies open like an oyster in the hand.

In Rome one day at Carnival a flour-
Bomb surprised me, covering me in white,
A proper suiting for the Church of Night,
If somewhat vulgar. Climb the tallest tower,
View any landscape here, its sepulture
Is cold retention, derogated, anal, dure.

De Quincey had my trouble – opium
For him; for me, inaction, looking on,
The bathroom stalled, the crucial moment gone.
The Bread of Culture, eaten crumb by crumb,
Chokes off all other appetite, and we
Who will one day be prints exist in effigy.

The picture of itself, the Great Good Land,
Which waits your passage in the sired boat,
Is not so truthful as a brother's coat,
Your many-coloured words. We understand
Each other who were not made here, but seek
The broad bestowing stream fed by clearskin creek.

The mail leaves town, I've often noted, by
The Porta Roma, wheels retarded, carrying
Enchantments far back home, the marrying
And dying, gossiping – this claimed life's wry
Postmark of ancient love and new device
Is Advent of Degree, point made, distinction nice.

Birds in the Garden of the Cairo Marriott

And you, little birds, are waiters but not smiling,
hopping at the sad indignity of that man
(he said Detroit was home) on his second
giant burger; with your quick in-and-out
besieging tables sweetened by the sugared sky
of Cairo, you mock the nicest men with napkins
on their shoulders – would they snap at scraps? –
and your big rivals, we'd call them crows
but they are dignity itself in brown tuxedos,
peering from high perches of a Disney Ramasseum,
speaking faultless American forever,
they must be Prefects of the Underworld!

The little dust we drop our crumbs upon
seethes like the Red Sea Crossing – if this is history,
asks a powerless nation, can mere birds
patrol the Valley of the Kings each morning?
Three sparrows who have 'hotep' somewhere
as a suffix drop beside our just uncovered
breakfast tomb: all food, they say,
is like another wave upon the Nile, a dream
worth sleeping for – the gods immured in obelisks
consider everything; their High Priests clad in aprons
are opening umbrellas as the sun begins
to climb above the masts of potted palms.

Ranunculus Which My Father Called a Poppy

The flower which gave Browning his worst rhyme
lined my Father's walk to his Paradise Garden
but he took his time.

Not for him the red of Flanders Fields sprung from
his Brother's body steeped in duckboard marl
nor the necrology of the Somme.

Defeat lived in those several petal folds,
that furry stalk and leaf, those half-drenched pinks
and shabby-borrowed golds.

This modest plant served what was mystical in him,
he'd banish eucalyptus yet cherish the paw-paw's
testicular seraphim.

So Europe and Australia grew together in the sun
of his waterless Eden – not snakes but sparrows
he'd kill, had he a gun.

A whole rift valley of regret ran its juiceless way
among the dahlias, salpiglossis, antirrhinums,
sufficient unto any day.

Later, his Nursing Home was steeped in garden gloom,
a shaven lawn devoid of flowers – for ten years
he surveyed it from one room.

Our front gate is open, I watch him hobble-kneed
sifting his inch-long plants from hessian – ranunculus
are hard to grow from seed.

Christmas Day, 1917

Was there fighting near Comines-Warneton that day?
I doubt there were minglings of combatants
In No Man's Land – it was one Christmas too many.
        But it might have been
A good day to die if ever there could be one.
He may have been wounded elsewhere; the salient
Had many names which guesswork could frequent,
        And hospitals between.

Eighty-nine years later two English schoolgirls
On a Flanders outing have used their new cameras
To record in pastel shades the headstone
        Of Private Neville Main.
Did I know my uncle's other name was Vivian?
I was given Neville in his memory. I joined the House
Of Names years after he had left it – not words, not vows,
        Just the invoiced pain.

How extraordinarily neat, well-spaced,
The Prowse Point Military Cemetery is –
How mistaken my memory of my family's memory
        Of these our far-off dead.
Two weren't even born where I thought they were,
My Mother must have been living still at home
When the news came, but she didn't die alone.
        My civilian Father did.

The valiant inscriptions, chiselled out
Or cemented in, the grass's mapping edges,
My Granddaughters' pictured sky, half-blue –
        Everything's still here.
A Belgian Christmas might well have seemed
Like the traditional ones transported to
Australia, though without the surf in view,
        The sun across the pier.

Time and place are real to the After-Dead
Though their inheritors have forgotten who they were.
Out of the plains of Europe come the tall Hussars
        Like brolgas massing.
As thoughts are lightweight, they can reach the sky.
Allow me, startled Uncles, these complaining words:
Both those who stay at home and those who serve
        Are posted missing.

The Violin's Obstinacy

It needs to return to this one note,
not a tune and not a key
but the sound of self it must depart from,
a journey lengthily to go
in a vein it knows will cripple it.
It would never have been born
if some fanatic touch of bow
and finger-board had not insisted –
it would have been the world
so timely unrevealed.
It would never have heard the E of deafness
or waded into the Rhine,
nor been required to watch
the conductor giving entries late.
So the note continues in its orbit
around its own elbow, playing musical chairs
with only one place to sit down,
its true death-bed. Like the trapped fly
in the window pane or the Abraham
of God's vindictiveness, it deploys
an endlessness of almost ending.

River Quatrains

You never step in the same river twice
Although it looks just as it did before.
Only a perfect stillness will suffice
To keep Narcissus seeing what he saw.

Our prisoners we like to send upriver.
We load our troopships many miles downstream.
We are the true side of the Guadalquivír,
The other is enemies of the regime.

Our City Fathers' planning is polite.
The abattoir is on the edge of town.
Yet out of mind may not be out of sight;
Here on, the river runs a darker brown.

The Boat Race passes just beneath our windows,
We hear them cheering different shades of blue.
We don't get up and rearrange our clothes,
We're in a boat that's crewed by only two.

When Caesar led his troops across the Rubicon,
They thought: 'This guy's no Marius or Sulla,
He's Number One,' and shouted out his song,
'I am the Very Hungry Caterpillar'.

Alaric the Goth commanded that
The Busento change its course to hide his tomb;
In Cosenza now only the bureaucrat
Disposes of the dust which conquered Rome.

The River Jordan flows in semiquavers,
The Seine runs on past Seurat's tingling dots,
The dead on Ganges ghats burn round the bathers,
The Acheron parts Haves from the Have-Nots.

How doubly bright our minor river shines –
Its Bankside boulevards, boutiques and bars,
Its tax-loss growers of designer wines,
Container mud beneath electric stars.

See them gather by the river – Johannes
Der Taufer preaching that Messiah is near.
But those white sheets and that well-knotted harness?
How long, how long, before some God appear?

I'm on a river bank. I think I see
The farther side: a choice of nothingness
Or Paradise. My poems wait for me,
They look away, they threaten and they bless.

The Downside

And the small exemplary lives
for which great cathedrals were constructed
are with us still. Here is the incinerator
your Father burned his leaves in –
there is the great book of the Inferno
where hate has a part for everyone,
perhaps you had a hand in it?
It goes on being written – on the other side,
as people say. Once you have a calling
you know you will be called for.

Opus 77

What works you did will be yourself when you
Have left the present, just as everything
The past passed to the present must become
A terrible unstoppable one blend
Of being there (the world) and not to be
(The self). Grow old along with me, the best
Is bet to be – the worst (of course) lack(s) all
Conviction, as the poet mistranscribed,
Storming a grave to satisfy his pride.
They love me, all my words, despite how often
I made fools of them, betrayed them, begged
Forgiveness of them. They are like the million grubs
Which swarm around their Queen. I file them in
Wide boxes where they wait their Master's Voice,
Accusing and defending. A letter plans
To burst in sullen flame, its heat conserved
By what was written once – but chiefly silence
Triumphs under missing banners – death
Will be the one unmentionable
Impossibility. What happened lives
Parenthetically and privately.

It is time to use words to transcend words,
To make a maquette of the ageing soul
Inside the tired body – abstract, oh
So abstract, but the mind anticipates a real
World trimmed like a Park of Dreams, where blood
Is its own sun and where the self is both
The quarry and the hunter. We who made

A better place with Art (if we did well
Or pointlessly) are privileged to bow
And leave and hope to find the courage to
Confront the mad god of the Universe
And honour one more time those rational
Constructions we have loved. No word will bear
A leaf, since we are dying in our roof-top pots;
Our after-lunch inseminations bring
Cries beneath our windows: we should be
Big enough to fit the act of ending,
The sprawling melodrama of Creation,
And be polite enough to stroll away –
None of that poetic braggadocio
Of buggering off quickly: he meant the body
Not the soul, but arrogance still thinks
The flesh will go on listening, and flaunts
The several litanies of Godhead. Be
Like Haydn abandoning his last quartet;
Need neither saving nor redeeming; greet
The world of breathing and the silent world
With the same material gesture – a bed-post
Now the herm of lost vicinity.

2010

After Schiller

Where was I and what then happened to me
When half-light moved beyond eclipse?
Didn't I foresee the end, and you agree
Love is the clumsiest of partnerships?

And would you wish to hear me speak to you
Of irretrievable darkness by the sea;
Of happiness too far off to travel to
And in some narrow space a leafless tree?

The sound of speech, the voice of sense on earth,
In this adjunct seems carpentered of years.
My richness now is nothing but a dearth
Of tricks for the wiping-away of tears.

Moving further, may I find again
The nub of things we shared – the bridal face
Whose hurt if mine was not mine to explain
But made to seem a human commonplace?

With looking upwards hardly in my power
And being forced to seek the stars on earth,
In this exacting planisphere I cower:
I have not moved one footstep from my birth.

Weightless in everlasting space, but true
To the blindly heavy rules of time,
I have become a harbinger for you
Of every weighted station of your climb.